The Novel Writer's Toolkit

■ ■ ■

From Idea to Best-Seller

Bob Mayer

http://coolgus.com

Copyright © 2003 by Bob Mayer, updated 2011

Revised Copyright © 2011 by Bob Mayer

ISBN-13: 9781935712299

Contents

Revised Edition

The original version of this book was published as **The Novel Writer's Toolkit:** *A Guide to Writing Great Fiction and Getting it Published* through Writer's Digest in 2003. At the time, it was the accumulation of 13 years of experience as a professional author. I am now entering my 22nd year in this business and have over 50 books that have been published traditionally as well as through my own publishing company: Who Dares Wins Publishing. The fundamental way I approach my writing has not changed that much over the years. I continue to plot, outline, research and follow techniques that have helped me hit the NY Times Best-Seller list and be one of the top-selling indie authors. However, one of the tenets of another book I wrote, **Write It Forward:** *From Writer to Successful Author*, is to be open-minded to new ideas. A writer must be willing to learn, grow and hone their craft in order to continue writing successfully.

Much of what has been added to this edition are elements that have changed my writing process. The new things I have learned through teaching, working with other writers and listening to those who have done what I want to do—write a better book.

This book focuses on the *craft of writing*. Content is king. Content is the foundation for everything you do as writer. This book will help give you the tools to hone your craft, write the better book, and ultimately achieve your goals.

I highly recommend you compliment this book with its sister book, **Write It Forward,** which is a training program to becoming a successful author. Where **The Novel Writer's Toolkit** covers developing our skills as an artist, **Write if Forward** develops our business savvy, and how to get published, and even self-publish, so we can be successful in the ever-changing world of publishing.

But first, you must write the better book. So let us begin.

Introduction

This book is the journey through developing an idea and turning it into story. I'm going to give you the tools that can help your manuscript rise above others in either the slush pile or the vast ocean of newly self-published books.

Most writing is not a special gift or talent. Writing is a skill that can be taught. It can be likened to bricklaying; you learn it one brick at a time, and you get better the more bricks you lay.

The key is to always be willing to learn, grow and develop these skills. A writer, in order to master their craft, must be willing to change.

If you talk to those who work in hospices, they'll tell you what lessons their dying patients bestow upon them. One word keeps coming up again and again: regret.

When faced with death, people look back over their lives. All the missed opportunities, the misplaced priorities, the things that weren't done. Only a handful of people focus on what they did do and are content. These people have negotiated the five emotional steps of change, which are Elizabeth Kubler-Ross' stages of Death & Dying. The last stage is acceptance. Kubler-Ross found that only 5% of those who were told they had a terminal illness were able to negotiate those five stages.

That number strikes a cord, because in my Write It Forward book, I refer to the 5% rule for internally motivated change. I've taught writing for decades and have always been shocked at how few writers actually change anything in their writing. I am no longer shocked. I have acceptance that I cannot change anyone but me. I can assist others if they desire it. This is based on my experiences and, more importantly, what I've learned from other writers, books, shows, and life.

78% of Americans believe they can write a book. I'd be willing to bet 77% of them will die regretting they never did. It's not about getting published. It's about creating and acting instead of reacting, often too late.

You have only one thing stopping you from writing the best book you are capable of. You.

This is a Toolkit because no tool is wrong. If I need to fasten two pieces of wood together and instead of picking up a hammer and nail, pick up a saw, it is not the tool's fault. It's mine.

I'm going to lay out numerous writing tools on these pages that will help you develop your craft as a writer. However, becoming an artist is up to you.

Point of view is the most critical style element in writing. It's also important in following the way I teach writing. I've been making a living writing for well over two decades and with each year and every new manuscript come new lessons learned. Over that time period I've taught writing novels and getting published at various workshops and for numerous organizations. I've attended many workshops and listened to other authors present. I've read many books and watched many movies and shows, constantly analyzing the writing, to learn new ways of creating. I've seen numerous ideas, stories and manuscripts in the course of teaching, helping other writers, and judging contests. I've been published by six different American publishers, many foreign publishers, worked with over two dozen editors, and have had four primary agents. I've been traditionally published by the Big Six in New York, and non-traditionally published through my own imprint. I've had hardcover, trade paperback, mass-market paperback, print on demand, and eBooks published across the range of possible platforms.

The words that follow are my experiences and opinions. They were born out of my desire to give those I taught something solid when they attended a seminar or class or bought a book.

Too many people lament the state of publishing and the "crap" that fills the shelves in the local bookstore or has been uploaded as an ebook. My goal in this book is not to complain but to explain; to tell you about the craft and art of writing so you can accomplish your goals.

The world of writing is a very diverse one and there is a place in it for just about everything and everyone. Things are changing rapidly, faster than ever, and I think it's an exciting time to be an author, with more opportunities than ever before.

The bottom line is *I write because I enjoy it*. That doesn't mean it's easy. The one commonality I have seen in every successful writer I've met is that they work very, very hard. There is a large degree of craftsmanship required to write a novel. It's not magic; it's hard work combined with the ability to constantly accept being critiqued and to critique one's self.

There's an advantage to the information in this book. It was written over the course of my writing career so you are going to get information written when I was tightly focused on craft, and you are also going to get information when I was tightly focused on the art of writing. Most writing books give you one or the other--here you get the whole deal. I've learned more about the craft of writing in this past year, my 22nd as a published author, than in all the years previous, because I've been more open to learning than ever before.

Additionally, in the last several years, I've focused on what it takes to be a successful author, not just in terms of the writing, but in terms of not only surviving, but thriving in the world of publishing. Most of that is in my **Write It Forward** program and book, but I will cover some of that here when it's needed.

The bottom line is the book. I love books. I love reading them and I love writing them. So if you love books, the words that follow are a glimpse behind the mysterious curtain of how they are born in the crucible of passion and idea, then written, and published.

I will take you step by step on the journey from original idea to the completed manuscript.

"I am always doing that which I cannot do in order to learn how to do it." Pablo Picasso.

Anything that upsets you, makes you feel bad, makes you angry, touches any emotional button is something you *must* focus on. We get upset whenever we hear or read something that affects us. Because we are hearing a truth, we react defensively with emotion. Our strongest defenses are built around our greatest weaknesses. As a writer, you will only get better by addressing the weakest parts of your writing. We all tend to want to focus on our strengths, but a book is only as good as the weakest part.

"I'm convinced fear is at the root of most bad writing." Stephen King

Often it is fear that keeps us from achieving our goals. It is fear that keeps us from writing. It is fear that stops us from living our inner dream. But fear is the seed of regret.

So. If you want to write, remember: No regrets.

Live your inner dream.

How To Use This Book

Read it through from start to finish to get the big picture, then go back and examine the parts. While I have broken this book down into tools, they are all interconnected. Just as a good novel has many loops that tie it together, so does this book. You have to study all the pieces, the tools, that I am laying out in front of you, and then try to put them all together in the large concept of not only writing a novel, but being a professional writer.

Tool 1: The Writer

The Common Traits of the Successful Writer

It's not normal to sit alone and write 100,000 words. So let's get that out of the way. You aren't normal. You aren't in the bell curve and you aren't necessarily on the good side of the curve. You're cursed. You write because you have to. You will have to go to therapy. Sorry. That's the reality of being a writer.

If you desire to write a novel because you want to have a best-seller and make a bundle of money, my advice is to play the lottery; it will take much less time and your odds will be about the same, if not better, and I can guarantee that the work involved will be much less. The publishing business makes little sense and it's changing faster than ever before. However, I do believe that the more you know, the greater your chances of success. The vast majority of writers are flailing away at the craft and the business blindly. Armed with knowledge, you greatly increase your ability to rise above the rest.

This book is focused on the **craft of writing**. As I mentioned earlier, how to be a successful author, selling your book and the business of writing is covered in my companion book **Write It Forward**. I believe it's important to have two separate books, because too often writers put the cart before the horse: business before craft. The first thing you must do as a writer is create a great book. This is a mantra that will be repeated throughout the nine tools.

You write for *you*. You write because you have a story in you that has to come out. This is the core of the art of writing. Pearl Buck said:

"The truly creative mind in any field is no more than this: a human creature born abnormally, inhumanly sensitive. To him a touch is a blow, a sound is a noise, a misfortune is a tragedy, a joy is an ecstasy, a friend is a lover, a lover is a god, and failure is death. Add to this cruelly delicate organism the overpowering necessity to create, create, create—so that without the creating of music or poetry or books or buildings or something of meaning, his very breath is cut off from him. He must create, must pour out his creation. By some strange, unknown, inward urgency, he is not really alive unless he is creating."

I believe that passion which fuels long-term perseverance to be *the single most important factor*. I also believe that *too much* discussion on the topic of creativity can actually stifle the drive in some people. They start thinking that they have to do and think exactly like everyone else in order to succeed and that is not true. That is why I say that there are no absolutes, no hard and fast rules in writing. Follow *your* path.

I have listened to many writers speak, read many books on writing, and while much of what they say is the same, there is often something that is very different. Usually that different thing is part of their creative expression, the way they approach their writing. However, on a core level, I think most creative people operate in a similar manner.

I see people who do something like #nanowrimo (National Novel Writing Month) where they try to write a certain number of words each day, every day and I have two views of that: it's good they are getting words down. But are they the type of writer who works that way? I know writers who don't write every day, but work in creative bursts. They might not write for a week, then knock out 20,000 words in three days. #nanowrimo doesn't work for them. Stephen King says he writes 10 pages a day. That's great for him. Does it work for you?

Additionally, that is what he *says*. Does he actually *do it?* Probably, but maybe not. He's the only one who knows the truth. Most writers feel a subliminal degree of guilt over getting paid to sit at home and create stories. So sometimes we says things to make it more apparent that we 'work'. Because it's hard to explain how hard it is to simply be sitting still, doing nothing, while we develop blinding headaches trying to work our way through our plot while remaining true to our characters. So we use things like word count and page count instead, even if they aren't true.

When I discuss how to write a novel, I talk a lot about the craft of novel writing. The art is woven into the craft with deeper insights and when you take craft and twist it by breaking rules. But the first rule of rule breaking is to know the rule. Thus we must learn craft before we look to art.

Craft is the intellectual aspect of writing. The art is the emotional aspect. A great writer engages both the reader's thoughts and emotions, thus being both a good craftsmen and a good artist.

One of the paradoxes of writing, and something to keep in mind when going through this book: I am going to present techniques, ideas and formats that are the *accepted* way of doing things; yet the *accepted* way makes you the same as everyone else who can read a writing book and follow instructions, and your work has to stand out from everyone else's. So how do you do that? How do you do things the *right* way yet be different?

Everything mentioned in this book is a template; do not allow anything to stifle *your* creativity. Remember the paradox. The best analogy I can come up with is that if you were a painter I am telling you about the paint and the canvas and lighting and perspective, but ultimately you are the one who has to decide *what* you are going to paint and *how* to paint it.

Another thing is to understand the techniques and methods, and then use your brilliance to figure out a way to change the technique or method to overcome problems and roadblocks. To be original—an artist—with something that's already been done. Also to mix techniques and methods in innovative ways.

I call this a **Writers' Toolkit** because if you pick up a hammer when you need a saw, that doesn't invalidate the hammer as a tool. It means you made a mistake as a craftsman.

The Basics
Write a lot
Before writing a lot, be a voracious reader

I also am a big fan of watching a lot of movies and TV specials and series. There are writers who dismiss the television, but there are great writers putting out excellent product in that medium. And we all can learn from any artistic medium. Studying a different medium can also allow you to see new ways of looking at your writing

Learn the proper way to do business things in the world of publishing such as having a strategic plan for your career, which is covered under my *Write It Forward* program and book

Why should you read this book rather than one of the many others books on the market about writing? I suggest that you read this in **addition** to those other works. However, the advantage of this book is that I began writing this book shortly after my first novel was accepted for publication in 1990 and have been adding to and modifying it ever since as we move into the second decade of the 21st Century. Thus this book presents a spectrum of my experience, not just my current experience.

In here you will find me writing in present tense about things that in real time happened years ago, but I've kept many of those passages because they offer insight from varying levels of my writing experience and thus give other writers at various levels more opportunities to connect their experiences with mine. I've learned more about writing in the past two years than in my first two decades because I've been more open to change.

If I wanted to be an architect I should not be satisfied that I only had grand visions of what the design for my buildings should be. Nor would anyone be impressed with my visions if I couldn't put them into the proper format. Nor would anyone be interested if my design was so impractical that it couldn't be built. I would have to learn the craft of design and also the business of building and then apply my vision to that. I would also need to understand how the people who actually construct the building operate, and interact with them in a professional and knowledgeable manner. And, perhaps most importantly and most often forgotten, I would not have any success if no one wanted to buy my designs.

Remember something about the art of writing: **It is the only art form that is not sensual.** You can see the colors and strokes that make a painting, feel a sculpture, and hear music. The manner in which each individual piece in those fields impacts on the senses is different. But every writer uses the same letters on a piece of paper. You have twenty-six letters that combine to form words, which are the building blocks of your sentences and paragraphs. Everyone has the same words, and when I write that word and you write it, that word goes into the senses of the reader in the same way. It's how we weave them together that impact the conscious and subconscious mind of the reader that makes all the difference in the world.

A book comes alive in the reader's mind. You use the sole medium of the printed word to get the story from your mind to the reader's. It is the wonder of writing to create something out of nothing. Every book started with just an idea in someone's head. Isn't that a fantastic concept?

Writers learn by writing. And before that, by being voracious readers.

In essence, writing is no different from any other profession. It's a simple rule, but one that every one wants to ignore: the more you write, the better you will become. Practically every author I've ever talked to, or listened to, or read about in an interview, says the same thing. I saw Stephen King on C-Span and he said the most important thing to do to become an author is to **write a lot**. One writing professor said you needed to write a million words before expecting to get published. I'm currently around word six million and still learning so much.

Let's look at the positive side: The odds are strongly against getting published. But simply by taking the time and the effort to learn from these words, you are increasing your odds. By continuing to write beyond your first manuscript, you vastly increase your odds. Many writers gush over the amount of money John Grisham made for *The Firm* but they forget that *A Time To Kill* was published previously to lackluster sales and failed. What is important to note about that was that Grisham realized he hadn't done something right and worked hard to change. Note that Grisham did not bemoan what his agent/editor/publisher etc. didn't do to help the novel. He didn't complain that the reading public didn't understand his brilliance. He worked on the one person he knew he could change: himself (a tenet of **Write It Forward**).

From talking with other published writers, I have found it is common that somewhere between manuscript numbers three and six, comes the breakthrough to publication. How many people are willing to do that much work? Not many, which is why not many succeed. But it is how you can vastly increases your chances of beating the odds. Publishers do not want to make a one-time investment in a writer. When a publisher puts out a book, they are backing that writer's name and normally want to have more than one book in the pipeline. Multiple book contracts are very common; with their inherent advantages and disadvantages. As soon as you type THE END on your first manuscript (and I mean THE

END after numerous rewrites), the first thing you must do is begin writing your second.

Publishing has changed drastically and there are new opportunities for writers to get their novels into the hands of their readers. Traditional publishing isn't the only viable option for the 21st century author. Self-publishing is quickly becoming the new medium for midlist authors, and new authors. Amanda Hocking self-published her way into a two-million dollar contract with St. Martins Press. Myself, Connie Brockway, Barry Eisler, LJ Sellers and JA Konrath have all either written ourselves out of NY contracts or turned down a NY contract and ventured out on our own and have been successful.

The key to our success is two-fold.
1. Write the better book
2. Become part of *Write It Forward*

I discuss what I would do regarding self-publishing for a new writer in *Write It Forward*, but suffice it to say, I believe you should have at least three manuscripts under your belt before venturing out there; not much different than getting traditionally published.

As someone who wants to be in the entertainment business, you have to study those who have succeeded and failed in that business. Read interviews with people in the arts and entertainment industries and you will find a common theme: a lot of years of sweat equity put in before the big "break" came. I've read of and heard actors and comedians talk about spending decades working in the trenches before they became famous. Musicians who sang backup for years before becoming lead. Painters who toiled in squalor (and often died) before their work was recognized.

Study the lives of writers. Read interviews with authors and see what they say. Go to conferences and talk to them. Listen to them talk about several things: how they became authors, how they live, how they feel about writing, how they write. Many worked very strange jobs before getting published. Almost all struggled and spent many years of suffering before they succeeded. I say suffering in terms of financial or career terms, not in terms of the writing itself. Most writers enjoy writing.

People seem to think that writers are different and, while in some highly publicized cases they are, most published writers have spent many years slugging away before their first novel was published.

Simple perseverance counts for a lot. I think many people with talent lack the drive and fall out of the picture and people with maybe not as much talent but more drive take their place. It's the difference between having a growth mindset and a fixed mindset. People with talent often believe they know all they ever need to know, therefore their mind is fixed. Those who believe there is always something more to learn, have a growth mindset.

Let's get back to where I talked about people in other professions doing a work practicum. Besides writing novels and reading, the other advice I would give would be to attend conferences and workshops. It is a worthwhile investment of your time and money to go to workshops and conferences. Not just to learn, but also to network. Because of that, the first Write It Forward 'short' my publishing company released is *How To Get The Most Out Of Your Time And Money At A Writer's Conference*.

A college student once interviewed me and she asked me what she could do to become a better writer. I replied with my usual "Write a lot," then thought for a second, looking at this nineteen year old woman. Then I said: "Live a lot. Experience life, because that is what you are eventually going to be writing about."

Think about the lifestyle of an author, the lifestyle you are hoping to achieve. Most people want the end result: a published novel in the bookstore or online, but they don't pay much attention to the life that produces that end result. A writer's life is one of paradoxes. You have to be interested in people, yet you work in one of the loneliest jobs there is and you are probably an introvert (extroverts rarely can sit alone long enough to produce 100,000 words). You need inspiration and passion, yet also possess the self-discipline to trudge through writing 400 pages of a manuscript. In other words you have to have a split personality and be slightly nuts. So you will need therapy and lots of it.

What Character Traits Do Successful Authors Share?

Patience And Self-Discipline

It takes a long time to write a novel. No matter how fast you are, it takes a while. In fact, while some things like NANOWRIMO on Twitter which has people writing at a furious pace for a month is good to get the writing down, it is also negative in that quantity is not necessarily quality.

The amount of time I spend writing a novel has actually increased the more I learn about the craft. Rather than making it easier, more knowledge makes it more difficult to write, as I try to make the book the best possible product I can.

Writers are often asked what their daily schedule is. I think it's important to have the discipline to have a daily schedule and/or goal. It's too easy to let the writing go and take care of everything else if you don't force yourself to face that daily goal.

It's different for many writers but here are some from writers I know:

5 pages a day; 2,000 words a day; 10 pages a day; six hours a day.

I think an external goal that can be measured is the best to go for. It's a tangible goal and you know when you've accomplished it. While this might seem to contradict the statement made above about something like NANOWRIMO, the key is that the work is often going back and layering onto writing already done.

Beyond that tangible writing goal, I work seven days a week, any-where from eight to fourteen hours a day. It's hard for me to say how many hours a day I work because I am almost always 'working'. If I'm not sitting in front of my computer, I'm researching or watching the news for interesting facts or simply thinking about my story, playing it out in my mind, watching my characters come alive. I have many of my best plot ideas while driving or riding my bike. Sometimes I wake up in the middle of the night with an idea, which is why I have my iPhone with recorder next to my bed ready for instant use.

My cable bill is very high, with every channel, on-demand, and DVR. There are writers who say 'kill your television' but I disagree with that. There's some very good writing in that medium. I watch movies and shows the same way I read books: analytically to see what the writers did and also what were the possibilities that weren't explored. The #1 thing a writer must do other than write is read and watch movies and shows. It is work. It will take away some of your enjoyment of things as you can get good at predicting what will happen next under Chekhov's rule of 'don't have a gun in act one unless you use it by act 3'. But note that I say 'use it' not 'fire it'. That's the key to great writing. To take what is expected and do the unexpected.

Writing *is* 99% perspiration and 1% inspiration. If you write only when excited or motivated you'll never finish. You have to write even when it's the last thing you want to do. Just put something down. You can always edit it later or throw it out (you'll do a lot of throwing out and it hurts but it's the sign of a mature writer; also, it's one reason you don't edit yourself to death on the first draft). I eventually average 500 to 550 pages of manuscript to produce 400 good pages in a final draft. A recent manuscript was 126,000 words long and then I cut it back to 90,000 words. To sweat over that many pages and then "lose" them hurts but not as much as getting the manuscript rejected or not sell if self-published. The longer I've written, the *more* I've become a fan of rewriting and editing. I'm also a fan of outlining and doing a lot of work before I write the first sentence of my manuscript, including doing extensive character development. This is a trait among several authors I've talked to. Both Terry Brooks and Elizabeth George got back lengthy editorial letters on the first book they sold. They determined then and there to make sure that future manuscripts would not require such rewriting. And they didn't.

Overall, I've developed an inner "writing clock" that works in terms of weeks and months that lets me know how much I have to produce and how quickly. It varies its pace depending on the project at hand and it took years of experience to develop this inner clock. I force myself to put the time and effort in, even when I don't feel like it. However, as I discuss in *Write It Forward*, almost every writer tends to underestimate the time it takes to complete a manuscript.

Experiment and find something that works for you in day-to-day writing. Maybe it will only be for one hour every morning before everyone else gets up—keep doing it. You'll be amazed how much you can get done if you stick with it. One rule that's hard for people is to TURN OFF THE INTERNET while writing.

Scott Turow wrote *Presumed Innocent* on the train to and from work in Chicago. Don't let circumstances stand in your way.

All the thinking, talking, going to writer's conferences, classes, etc. are not going to do you any good if you don't do one basic thing: WRITE.

When I taught martial arts, I always found that the majority of the new students quit right after the first month. They came in and wanted to become Bruce Lee rolled into Chuck Norris all within a couple of weeks. When they realized it would take years of boring, repetitive, very hard work, the majority gave up. It doesn't take any special skill to become a black belt; just a lot of time and effort to develop the special skills. The same is true of writing. If you are willing to do the work, you will put yourself ahead of the pack. You must have a long-term perspective on it. Under *Write It Forward*, your strategic plan, in essence, is where do you want to be in five years as a writer?

I think a hard part of being a writer is also knowing what exactly 'work' is. For me it was hard to accept that kicking back and reading a novel was work and I wasn't being a slacker. Sitting in a coffee shop and talking with someone is work. Living is work for a writer in that you can only write what you know, so therefore experience is a key part of the creative process.

Ultimately, though, as Bryce Courtney says, you need a large dose of *bum glue*. Gluing yourself to that seat and writing.

The Ability To Organize

As those pages pile up, you'll find yourself weeks, months, maybe years away from having written that opening chapter. That's where your organizing skills come in. We'll cover outlining later on, but in essence, the way you organize your life, is the way you will initially organize your book. So if your life is all over the place, you might have some problems. Yes, there are those natural talents who can just 'stream' a book, but they are few and far between. Most of us cannot keep an entire book in our head.

You have to keep track of your characters, your locales, and the action, to make sure it all fits. I've used many different tools to write a novel, but one thing I've done with every single manu-script is use what I call a **story grid**. This is an Excel spreadsheet where I can put the entire book on one page, scene by scene (for a really big book it might go to two pages). This spreadsheet is not an outline (I will cover outlines in Tool 3), but rather something I fill in with a pen each day as I write, to help me keep track of what has been done. Every day I then update the spreadsheet and print it out. It sits to the left of my keyboard (I'm left-handed). It helps when you need to go back and look up a specific part or change something. I will discuss the story grid in greater detail in **TOOL 3**.

I also keep numerous indexed binders with all my research mate-rial handy. I spend a considerable amount of time organizing my research material so I can find what I'm looking for. Details drive a story, and the more details you have accessible in terms of research, the more options you have in your plot. Right now I have two four-inch thick binders: one for people; one for events.

Some writers use programs like Scrivener or Onenote to keep track of their research, but I'm still old-fashioned and use Word and Excel and binders.

An Active Imagination

A novel is a living, active world you invent. Imagination is essential.

In some ways a novel is like a chess game in that you have to be able to think half-a-dozen to a dozen steps ahead for all of your pieces (characters) while at the same time considering what the other guy might be doing (the limitations of your plot; the point of view chosen to present the story, etc.). You have to pick the successful moves and the correct strategic direction given a very large number of variables. But you are also limited by the personality of the characters you've invented—they have to act within the 'character' you have given them, much like each chess piece is capable of only a certain type of move. It's your imagination that allows you to thread the proper path. And in most cases, there are numerous "all right" paths, but one stands out above the others as the "best" path and finding the "best" one is critical.

The Mind

Yeah, you do sort of need one to be a writer. I'd like to say a little bit more about the mind for two reasons: one is that it is the primary tool you use when writing. Second, to write good characters, you need to understand the mind because it's the driving force behind your characters' actions.

As a "machine" the brain is very inefficient. Physiological psychologists estimate that we use less than ten percent of our brain's capabilities (rent the Albert Brooks movie *Defending Your Life* and see how he uses this in his story). In many ways, that is what makes writing fiction so hard and draining: you are trying to expand the portion of your mind that you normally use and tap into your subconscious. A little bit of understanding of that other 90 or so percent is useful. It is commonly called the subconscious or the unconscious and plays a very large role in determining our character (key buzz word). Whether you agree with people such as Freud and Jung, it is useful to know a little bit about their theories. A fully rounded character has a complete brain and while they may only consciously be using ten percent, that other ninety percent affects their actions.

As a writer you will start having dreams about your story and your characters. That's your mind working even when you consciously aren't. You will also run into *writer's block,* which I believe, when real, is your subconscious telling you to hold until you realize in your conscious mind something important with regard to the story. This is where the "write what you feel" school of creative writing comes in. I believe what they are focusing on is this very thing: the power of the subconscious (90% vs. 10%). It is more than feeling though; it is a large part of your brain and the better you can get in touch with it and use it, the better your writing will be.

There are many experiences a writer should have in order to understand both their own mind and the minds of other people. You have to remember that you are not the template for the rest of humanity. Hard as it may be for some to believe, there are differences between people.

I've sometimes said the best thing about a writers' group is not necessarily the critiquing or networking, but rather watching the different 'characters' in the group and trying to figure out what is motivating them to act the way they do.

If you don't understand yourself both mentally and emotionally, you might have a hard time understanding others. Therapy can be a very useful tool to help a writer dig into their own mind to figure out where they are coming from. Later in this book where I discuss what to write about, a critical question I think a writer should know the answer to is: Why are you writing this novel?

After listening to many authors speak of their creative processes I realize they are talking on two levels. There's what they are saying and there is what they are meaning. The saying part often varies, but they almost always mean the same thing. For example, there is the issue of outlining. I know writers who swear by outlining and others who say they don't outline at all, they just write. However, I've also found those who don't outline tend to do a lot of rewriting, thus the first draft of their manuscript might be considered a very detailed outline. Those writers who do a lot of outlining tend to not want to do much rewriting. But in the final analysis, although the two methods seem very different, they are actually the same in creative essence.

Also remember that there are two sides to the brain. The right side is your creative part while the left is more analytical and logical—this is where the editor part of you resides. Sometimes you have to silence that editor while creating or else nothing will get done.

Contentment & Desire

I started this book by saying wanting to make a million dollars isn't the best motivation to write a novel. But you do need some tangible reasons. In a perfect world I suppose we could accomplish all the things we would like without having any external stimulus. But this isn't a perfect world. I find putting my back against the wall helps. I wrote my first two novels living in Korea. I studied and taught martial arts six hours a day and went nuts the rest of the time. I wrote, to a certain extent, to keep my sanity. Then after getting published, I wrote because I enjoyed it but also to make money to live on. I had job offers where I could be financially secure, but I didn't take them. I wrote, and continue to write, because I have to both internally and externally.

No one wants to talk about money. I remember watching the movie *White Palace*. In it the character Susan Sarandon plays is having a relationship with a younger man and she goes with him to his apartment for the first time. She's very impressed with it and asks him how much he pays a month. He equivocates and hems and haws.

She looks at him and says something to the effect of: "We can sleep together and make love, but you won't tell me how much you pay for your apartment?" (I think her language wasn't as mild, though.) That comment struck me because it's so true of our society. Talking about money is more taboo it seems than talking about sex. I find this particularly interesting when we consider the academic side of writing. I was sitting in a writer's group that I helped form and we had invited a professor who edited the local university's literary publication to talk to us about the magazine. He started out by making the comment, "If you think you can make a living writing, forget about it." Be careful of bitter people because their aura can be damaging.

Because you can make money writing. I've done it now for over twenty years and am currently making more as an indie author than I ever made as a best-selling traditional author. I've heard some authors and freelancers say never give away anything you've written for free, even if just to see it in print, and I tend to agree. If someone isn't willing to pay for it, then work harder to make it good enough so someone will. Quite honestly, publishers will not be impressed with your credentials of getting published in publications that they never heard of and didn't pay you anything other than to give you three free copies. I'm not saying absolutely don't do that, but if you do, realize it is only a step and you need to move beyond. Don't get stuck there.

I am not saying write simply for the money, but if you don't factor money into the writing equation somewhere, and take it as a serious factor, you will fail, because eventually you will have to get a *real* job. Money cannot only be a source of motivation, but it is the basis for making a living at writing, which is very hard to do. It's a vicious equation: to become a better writer, you must write—to write you must have time to write—to have time to write it most certainly helps to make some money at it.

OK, now that I've gotten the mercenary side of the business out of the way, go back to Pearl Buck's quote: the root of your desire must be a passion to tell a story. Some people tend to look down upon telling a story in a format such as science fiction or mystery or action/adventure. But if that's your passion and your story, then tell it and don't worry what anyone thinks. I think there is one bottom line on how good a writer is: how many people read his/her book. That's called *commercial* writing and sneered at in certain quarters, but if no one wants to read what a person writes then maybe he or she just isn't writing that well. Think about it.

I sat on a panel at a conference and they asked each of us what we liked and disliked about writing for a living. The answers were interesting. I think an author needs the paradoxical combination of being able to be content and discontent at the same time. Because publishing is such a slow business and positive feedback so rare, you have to be reasonably content for long periods of time by yourself. At the same time you have to motivate yourself to write the manuscript, to do all the dirty work that needs to be done, to pursue long-range goals.

Setting Objectives

So far I've talked about what you need. Now let me mention something we could all do without: procrastination. If you're like me, when you were in school, that term paper never really needed to be done until the night before it was due. I remember at West Point the radio station would have a contest the night before the big Social Sciences paper was due. They would have call-ins with the award going to the person who could claim they were starting their paper the latest.

In fact, for me, the one time I did a paper early—in fact so early that I was able to get feedback without a grade—the instructor gave me some basic pointers which I incorporated, then turned in the paper—again early, this time for a grade. I got an F. So much for positive reinforcement.

My main theme is that to become a writer you must write. You can be the greatest marketing specialist in the world, but if you don't have a product to market, you're not going to get published or sell. I am very big on understanding the business aspects of publishing and marketing your work as best you can, but I have seen people (including myself at times) forget one very important rule: you have to have a good product. Putting ninety percent of your effort into trying to sell your work when it is simply not good enough, is a waste of time. Put that effort into writing another manuscript that is good enough.

The best way I've found to overcome procrastination is to set objectives, both short and long range. I cover this in detail under the first **TOOL: WHAT** in *Write It Forward.*

If you feel such cold objectives interfere with your creativity, you might be right. But a novel is a heck of a long way to go simply burning the fuel of passion. One common fault that many suffer from is starting a novel, getting about a quarter of the way in, then dropping it to move on to something *better*, and starting a new novel. I know in everything I've worked on, about a hundred and fifty pages in, my mind has already started to move on to a new project and I'm somewhat bored with what I am working on. That's where discipline and a schedule come in. If my next project isn't due to start for three more months, then I have to work those three months on my present project in order to earn the right to start the new one.

Open-Mindedness

You could also call this *willingness to change*. This is not only important when starting out, but it is perhaps even more important after first getting published. You should be willing to learn from any source to improve your writing.

Before you can be willing to change though, you have to be willing to say the three hardest words in the human language for most people, "I was wrong". This should be followed with:, "Maybe I'm not doing this the best possible way. Maybe I can learn from someone else."

One thing I see too much of is writers who want validation instead of help. They want to be told how great their manuscript is and have a publisher put the check in the mail. They don't want to hear what's wrong and what more work needs to be done. I find this very strange in the environment of conferences and classes, where the entire purpose is not validation but to become better writers.

After three books published, I took some graduate literature courses at the local college. It was a very worthwhile experience and expanded my horizons. In fact, the longer I write, the more I appreciate the literary side of the house. I think many genre writers get too caught up in the "formula" of their genre and trap themselves, becoming unable to write anything different. In the same manner, if you have a background in literature, don't turn your nose up at information that seems too "common" or genre oriented.

I read a book and took a course on screenplays and learned some things about writing that I can incorporate not only into my work on screenplays, but also my novels. I found the way a screenplay is broken down interesting and I use it later in this book to help you get the big picture on how a novel works.

I recently watched the visiting writer at a local college come into our writer's group to do a reading. She walked in, did her reading, took her applause, and then walked out. I guess she was simply too good of a writer to waste her time listening to the other people in the group read or discuss writing. She didn't bother to find out whom she had just read to and because of that she lost the opportunity to network with several published authors who might have helped *her* in her attempts to publish her next novel.

That's another lesson I've learned—you never know who you're dealing with so be courteous and open to all you meet. No matter what your mindset, listen to others and what they have to say about writing even if you disagree with them. You might find yourself agreeing a year or two later. In this book, you might find me appearing to be somewhat schizophrenic, taking several different perspectives, some of them seemingly opposed to each other, but remember, I began writing this in 1990 and have been adding to it ever since, so in these pages you see some of my own evolution as a writer. I do have to say that for mainly ego reasons, I was very touchy when first starting out at what I perceived to be *snubs* from the literary community toward genre writing. Now I see that attitude to be naive and wrong. You have to decide what *you* want to do and pursue it, regardless of what others say or believe. Another thing I have learned is that it is guaranteed that someone, somewhere, will not like what you've written after you get published. It's also guaranteed that some of those people feel a burning desire to inform you of those dislikes.

The biggest change I have made over the years is to alter my perspective on plotting and characters. I will discuss this in detail further in this book but for my first dozen manuscripts or so I believed that the plot drove the story. Now I realize that characters drive the story. In order to make that change, though, I had to admit that what I was doing was not the best way to work and be willing to look at points of view diametrically opposed to my own.

You can't ever get better if you don't first admit you're not doing it the best possible way. When I taught a writing correspondence course, I would have to say that 80-90% of the students were unwilling to change anything based on the feedback I was giving them. The first question this raises is why they even took the course in the first place? The answer I mentioned above—they wanted validation. The few who did change, who did the hard work and reworked their material, and put the time into thinking about the questions I would pose—they made great strides as writers.

Remember that change takes stages. First one has to accept that there is a need for change. Then you have to intellectually accept the change, which isn't total acceptance. After a while of living with the mental acceptance, you will gradually have emotional acceptance of the change, which is total acceptance. That is why it takes years and years to change, if one ever does.

I find change usually requires Kubler-Ross's five emotional stages. I also touch on this in editing, but very briefly we tend to go through:

1. **Denial.** There is no problem or need to change
2. **Anger.** How dare someone, including me, say I'm not doing it right
3. **Bargaining.** Maybe if I can change some small things it will make a big difference
4. **Depression.** Yes, I do really need to change
5. **Acceptance.** Which leads to change

Once, I spent every day of a week reading the fifteen New York Times bestsellers. I did this because I wanted to become a NYT bestseller. I read them with an open mind and I learned many things. I adjusted some of the structure of my plotting in accordance with what I learned and incorporated what I learned in places in this book also.

There are two types of books, besides bestsellers, that I recommend new novelists read: first novels (because this book was sold on its own merits) and breakout novels (the book that breaks a mid-list author into being a best selling author).

I constantly have to reinforce to writers the fact that the reader does not know what the writer knows. That a writer must be able to get out of their own head and into the head of a reader who is starting from page one.

If you start your manuscript with fifty pages of expository material, knowing that your great hook is on page 51, realize one thing— the reader doesn't know the great hook is on page 51 and very few will want to wade through that much background information without knowing *why* it is important or that the hook is coming.

The Writing Routine

It seems like people always want to know what a writer's "routine" is. I always get that question when I teach and I always have a hard time answering it. I have the same sort of answer when people ask about some of the material in the next chapter: I will use and do whatever it takes to get a manuscript done. If I have to outline on an easel pad, I do it. If I have to write in chalk on the side of an apartment building, I'll do it. If I have to call the homicide squad to ask a stupid question, I'll try to get someone else to do it, and when they won't, do it myself.

Each individual has to discover what works, but the operative word in this sentence is *works*. Don't lock yourself in—find what works, and if it stops working, find something else.

One interesting thing I have found is that the entire creative process has many paths but they all seem to parallel each other. I listened to a panel with Terry Brooks, Elizabeth George, Bryce Courtenay and Dan Millman as each talked about their own unique process of writing a novel. And on the surface it appeared that all were very different in their approach, but underlying what they were saying, I could see that they all did essentially the same things, just differently. Confusing? For example, Terry Brooks is a big fan of outlining and hates rewriting. But Bryce Courtenay doesn't outline, he just starts writing and then spends a lot of time rewriting. But in essence, Bryce Courtenay's first draft of the manuscript is equal to Terry Brooks polished outline. The same thought processes and amount of work go into it.

Passion

This is what *you* feel about what you are writing about. I talk about intent a little further on—what you want the reader to feel from the book. You also have to consider how *you* feel about what you are writing, because consciously or subconsciously, it will come through in your writing.

Your passion could be to tell an interesting and entertaining story. It could be to write a novel about what love means to you. Sometimes when I am trying to get a writer to get back to their original idea, I ask them what is most important about their book to them? What do they feel the most about? This is the core of the book.

I refer to this throughout this book, but one thing I believe is that if you are a writer, no one can stop you from writing.

This brings up the difficult subject of rewriting and changing. I've seen writers totally change their manuscript based on the off-hand comment of an editor/agent/writing instructor. Sometimes the change is for the better, but sometimes it tears the guts out of the book. I think a writer has to be true to himself or herself first. But the writer also must be objective enough to get out of their own head and see if what they have written works. To have these two capabilities reside inside of one person is a paradox and why it is difficult for most people to do this successfully.

1 of N does not equal N *And* Never Complain, Never Explain

Arrghhh. Math in a writing book. Sorry, but it's the best way I can explain this concept. What this formula means is that just because you can go to the bookstore and buy a best-selling book written by so-and-so, the famous writer that does not mean you can write a similar book and get it published.

Ahh, now you're really mad at me. I'm contradicting what I wrote earlier. No, I'm not. What I'm talking about is those people who sit there and complain that their book is just as good as such and such and, damn it, they should not only be published but have a bestseller. Also, those people who look at book number 5 from a best-selling author and complain about how bad it is. Yes, there are many book number 5's from best-selling authors that if they were book number 1 from a new author, would not get published. But the primary thing that sells a book is the author's name. I've always said Stephen King could write a book about doing his laundry and it would be on the bestseller list. Stephen King earned being Stephen King and to misquote a vice-presidential debate,

I've read Stephen King and you ain't no Stephen King. Neither am I.

Another thing people do is they see a technique used in a novel and use the same technique, and then get upset when told it doesn't work. They angrily point to the published book that has the same technique and say, "SEE." Unfortunately, what they don't see is that that technique is part of the overall structure of the novel. It all ties together. I'll discuss book dissection to study various aspects and techniques and I still stand by that; however, I also remind you of the story of Frankenstein. Just because you can put all the pieces together, that doesn't mean you can necessarily bring it to life. There are some techniques that only work when put in context of other parts of the novel; thus using it in isolation can be a glaring problem. You can't take the beginning of one bestseller, tie it in with flashback style from another, and have a similar flashy ending as another and expect the novel to automatically work.

Every part of a novel is a thread connected to all the other parts. Pull on one piece and you pull on them all. Tear apart a novel or a movie and see the pieces, but then be like a watchmaker and see if you can put them all together again as the writer did and if you understand *why* they go back that way.

For example, Quentin Tarrantino ignored the classic three act screenplay structure with *Pulp Fiction*. Yet the movie was a great success. So therefore, a number of new screenwriters decided they didn't need the three act structure. However, what they failed to see is that it was not so much the unique story structure that made *Pulp Fiction* such a success, but rather the intriguing dialogue. Tarrantino's structure without the Tarrantino dialogue would have spelled failure.

It is also more important to figure out what is working and why, rather that what you feel didn't work in a book you read. An attitude that will serve you little good is the *there's so much crap on the shelves in the bookstore*. I admit that there are times when I am looking for something to read, and I stand in the local supermarket looking at the paperbacks, that I really can't find anything I want to read or that sparks an interest. But that doesn't automatically mean it's all crap.

I had to do this many times. I'd read something I might not like, but it seems to be selling quite well. Instead of dismissing the rest of the world as stupid, I try to find what it is about the book that people like. That doesn't mean I'm going to do the same thing, but it does broaden my horizon.

I don't think there is anything wrong with a little fire burning deep inside believing you are better than those people getting published, but I think that's the sort of thing that should be used to fuel your writing, not expressed loudly so everyone can hear it.

John Gardner once said that every book has its own rules. Remember that when you examine a book to see what you can learn from it. Look at the parts from the perspective of that book's specific rules.

I think Henry Ford uttered the famous line: **Never complain, never explain.** This applies in the writing world in several ways.

One thing I do when critiquing material is ask a lot of questions. I tell my students, 'You don't have to answer those questions to me' (in fact I would prefer they don't), but rather they are to get the students to think. What I don't tell them is that the more questions I have to ask, the worse job they've done.

The reason I don't want answers is because you don't get any opportunities to explain your book once it's on the shelf in a store. You also don't get any opportunities to explain your submission when it's sitting on an agent's or editor's desk. So if they don't "get it" the first time around, they won't *get it*. Get it? All your explanations and defenses mean nothing because you not only won't get the chance to say them, you *shouldn't* get the chance to say them.

I've gotten five page long, single-spaced letters back from students answering my questions or challenging points I made and my reaction is that such letters are a waste of paper. If I couldn't figure it out from the material, it needs to be rewritten. This ties in with my theory about the original idea. If you can't tell me what your story is about in one, maybe two sentences, *and* I understand it from that, then you are going to have a hell of a hard time selling it. You don't get to put those letters in the front of your published book. You must incorporate those answers in the novel itself through rewriting.

The never complain comes from the fact that there are people running this business. You won't agree with some things, particularly rejections, but do not complain or write nasty letters, make obnoxious phone calls, send dirty faxes, etc. etc. Because you never know when you are going to run into those people again. My first book was published by a publisher that had rejected my own query reference for that same book. I had disagreed strongly with some of the things they put on that first rejection letter, still do as a matter of fact, but I ate it and drove on. If I had sent them a nasty letter, methinks they would have remembered me and not even considered the manuscript when my agent submitted it.

I even find this with students I've worked with. They get angry and upset with my comments or questions. And they let me know it. What they don't understand is the fact that their anger expressed that way will get them nowhere. Take the energy and put it into your book, which is the only place it will do you any good.

Agent Richard Curtis' first piece of advice in his book *Beyond the Bestseller* to writers consists of a few simple words, "Keep your big mouth shut."

The longer I have been doing this for a living, the more I realize the profundity of those words. Go ahead, laugh. But here is the golden rule that I take out of those words: If an action you plan to take, words you plan to utter, a letter you want to write, an email you want to send, could have anything other than a positive reflection back on you, DON'T DO IT. Negativity begets negativity. Acting out of anger, frustration, righteous indignation, etc. will bite you in the butt, to put it mildly.

It is hard sometimes not to react. I believe publishing is a very poorly run business in many aspects. And those bad business decisions in New York can adversely affect you. They can destroy you in some cases. But you have to drive on and you have to accept that you, by yourself, are not going to change the entire publishing industry. Also, you can take comfort, if you want, in the fact that the business is in the throes of change.

At one publishing house, I went through five editors over the course of three years. I've had half-a-dozen people assigned to me as my *publicist*. None of my publicists returned my phone calls for the first two years. For my most recent book from that publisher my assigned publicist never even bothered to give me a courtesy phone call to tell me all the things they weren't going to do to promote the book.

For the same publisher I submitted an outline for my next book. I asked for feedback on the outline and received none. So I wrote the book and turned it in. Then I got a phone call a couple of weeks later saying the book didn't go in the direction they envisioned for my series. Was I angry? Yes. My gut reaction was to tell them it would have been good to have heard that when they sat on the outline for half a year, *before* I wrote a book that faithfully followed the outline.

What did I do? I kept my mouth shut and listened. And I realized that, ultimately, they were right. The book was going in the wrong direction. I spent three weeks, seven days a week, totally rewriting the manuscript and produced basically a new book. It sucked doing that. I didn't get paid any more money for doing it. But what were my options? Scream and yell and rant and rave? And then what? And, getting back to admitting you're wrong, their way was better than the way I had been going.

Most of the time, I have found that comments made by editors and agents, even when I very much disagreed with them initially, turned out to be very worthwhile. I never respond to anything right away. I always take some time to digest it.

At the same time, with the same publisher, they screwed up my royalty check (and it was *their* mistake) and issued it two weeks late, which almost cost me the closing date on the house I was trying to buy; plus the check was short money they owed me. Did I call up my editor and scream? No. I sent a polite letter detailing the situation to my agent and sucked it up.

I'm not saying be a patsy. Or go along with every single thing you are told. But I am saying don't shoot yourself in the foot and understand reality. They didn't sit there at the publishing house and decide to screw up the royalty check on purpose, even though paranoid people like us writers like to believe such things. On the flip side of that, though, I do believe you have to be persistent on your own behalf. No one is going to care more about your book than you.

For example, I am often asked how long a writer should wait to hear back on a query/submission to an agent or publishing house. My answer: Forever.

I'm not being a smart-ass with that answer. Rather I am defining the reality of the situation. What are you going to do if you don't hear back in two months? Send *another* letter or email to be ignored? Move on.

I said above that publishing is poorly run, but that doesn't mean the people who run the business are incompetent. Like many other businesses, publishing goes through changes and it takes time for bureaucracies to catch up to change.

One of the bitter realities of being a writer is that you have very little leverage. If something isn't happening the way you would like, there is little you can do. In the past year, several major writers, flagship writers who carry publishing houses—who have leverage—have switched publishers. They didn't do it over money, they did it over the way they perceived the publisher was treating them. How much publicity effort they were getting.

I stated earlier that this is an emotional business. If you want to succeed you need to have positive emotions working for you. This is very difficult for many writers. I switched agents because the original agent I had, while good, was a little too negative. I realized I had enough negative traits on my own (as you can see by reading between the lines on some of these pages). I didn't need my agent to amplify my negativity. I switched to an agent who is more confident and positive. Who also, coincidentally, is the most professional individual I've worked with in this business as far as correspondence and doing what he says he's going to do. However, he also doesn't 'hold my hand'. He expects me to be a professional and deal with the emotional issues of this business on my own. But he is also like a psychologist in that he leaves me alone a lot to figure things out on my own after giving me a few comments to chew on. Many people want the 'answer' right up front, but they don't realize they're not ready to accept the answer yet. In the same manner there are things in this book that you intellectually understand, but emotionally disagree with. I have often found that the things I most strongly react to with negative emotions are the things I need to pay most attention to.

Be positive.

I wrote the above two paragraphs two years ago. Since then I left that second agent to move on to a new agency. That's not to say there was anything wrong with that agent. However, I received advice from fellow writers, people who I respected, about what they felt would help my career and I listened to them, digested how I felt about the validity of their comments, and eventually followed their advice. It was difficult to do, since I had no burning reason to make the change, but in retrospect it was the right move.

And since I wrote the previous paragraphs, I've broken from NY publishing and struck out on my own. Despite all that, the craft of writing is the same.

Another aspect of this comes whenever you read a book or see a movie. Stop trying to find what's wrong with it and try to figure out what is working. It's easy to be a negative critic—much harder to find the elements that were successful. I believe that learning to do this was a significant achievement for me. I used to look at some best-selling novelists and think their work was totally worthless. Because of that, I failed to look hard enough to see the things in that work that *were* worthwhile and well done.

I recently got a letter from a student where the student first told me all the things he *didn't* like. He didn't like thrillers. He didn't like horror. He didn't like serial killer books, etc. etc. etc. My first reaction was why is this guy telling me this? Second, what good is it doing him to know what he doesn't like? Third, some of what he doesn't like could teach him a lot about writing. Fourth, he was telling me, in so many words, he didn't like what I wrote. Not a good way to start a working relationship.

The bottom line is I've learned to shut my mouth even if I have to bite my tongue in half to do it.

What a Writer Needs

Like any other profession, there are tools the writer uses. Here are some you need to consider.

A Laptop

Tolstoy's wife copied six drafts of *War And Peace* in freehand for him as he wrote it. Since most of us aren't as lucky to have such an understanding spouse/friend, a computer/laptop is almost indispensable. My hat is off to those legions of writers who produced their works before the day of electronic *cut* and *paste*.

Laptops are wonderful as you can take your work with you when you travel. I tend to get a lot done waiting for planes, trains and ferries. I purchased an adapter for my laptop that plugs into the cigarette lighter in my car, which allows me to charge my battery while on the road which increases my working capability. I haven't yet learned the trick of writing while driving and am not sure I will attempt that feat.

But I have been known to tap out some thoughts and ideas on the ferry from my remote island off the coast of Seattle. If it's a really great idea (they always are) I've been know to key it in at a rest area.

I used to do quite a few book signings at military post exchanges throughout the country. This consisted of sitting in front of the PX for twelve hours at a time trying to sell my books. I spent a lot of that time at the keyboard of my laptop, tackling two jobs at the same time. I carry an extension cord as part of my standard equipment in my brief-case so that I can plug in.

Most computers nowadays are much more powerful than what you need, capable of making phone calls, balancing your household budget, finding you a life partner on the Internet, doing the laundry and a whole list of other tasks—all you need is something with a key-board that will allow you to save what you write.

Always, always, always, and always, back up your work. And do it often. Nothing is more agonizing than to lose pages you have just written because of a mechanical malfunction or a power loss. I was in an interesting position writing my first couple of manuscripts in Korea. The power there would cut out at the strangest times and I learned to hit the keys for save almost automatically at the end of pretty much every paragraph.

I keep the latest copy of what I'm writing on my hard drive and back it up on a neat device called a time machine. It's automatic and I don't even have to think about it, except I check to make sure it is working every day. I also have a 32gig thumb drive on my keychain and I backup my important material every few days.

I also started using Dropbox, which is in the *cloud*. What is nice about Dropbox is I can park this master document there, share the folder with others, they can pull it up, edit it, and park it right back there for me to go over. Sure, you can do that in email, but this makes sure we are both working off the most recent document.

Besides, you never know, my home may catch on fire and the computer and time machine may be destroyed. Paranoid? Slightly, but I know there's someone out there who lost everything when they thought it was backed up.

Can't I simply write on legal paper with a pencil? Someone might ask. Certainly. If that's the way you write best. I read an interview with Joyce Carol Oates and she does her first draft with pen and paper. I've heard that some authors dictate their stories into a recorder and then transcribe it. Whatever works best for you.

A place to write

This is very individualistic. I like quiet most of the time, so I have an office in my home where I can close the door and focus on my writing. You will also need plenty of room to lay out pages and research along with a bulletin board to keep that list of characters and key information posted where you can constantly refer to it.

My work area has expanded over the years. Currently I have a large wraparound desk with over nine feet of length, a large four space file cabinet, two window sills full of books, five steel shelves holding various materials, two ceiling high bookcases, several vertical files, two cork bulletin boards, a dry-erase board, etc. etc. The bottom line is that I need plenty of area and I like to keep my work as organized as possible.

Some people like to grab pencil and notepad and curl up in bed. Others climb a mountain and like to write on the peak. Again, whatever works best and is within your realm of possibilities. I'm writing this paragraph sitting in my car waiting for the next ferry to take me to America. That is what we call it when we actually have to leave our peaceful little island and head to Seattle to make the Costco run. I'm a firm believer in using time wisely and my time is very valuable.

A Dictionary

And yes, I have seen cover letters with words misspelled. One thing I have learned is that although I may think I know what a word means, occasionally I am wrong. Sometimes it pays to look it up and know exactly what you are saying.

A friend of mine walked out to her sporty convertible outside a store and found a note stuck on her windshield. Some guy who had been eyeing her in the store had left it. She opened it up and read:

"Let's meat." And then listed his phone number.

Needless to say they didn't meat. Spelling is important.

A Thesaurus

Spell checks and thesaurus programs that come with your word processing software are not all that great. They can be helpful and useful, but sometimes a word is on the tip of our tongue, we know what it means, so we can look at the Thesaurus to find it.

The Synonym Finder by J.I. Rodale is a great resource. However, a word of caution. Don't rely on these books to find the right words or to find *bigger* words. I've seen many misused words or words that toss me from the reading solely because a writer was trying to be creative.

A Recorder

This tool can be helpful to put thoughts down when driving or you're in a position where you can't write. I also place mine by the side of my bed at night and when I wake at three in the morning with that brilliant idea, I mutter it into the recorder and play it back in the morning when my cognitive functioning is somewhat better. The most used app on my iPhone is the iRecorder.

I also record workshops where a group is brainstorming, because often someone says something and it's lost in all the conversation. With the recording, we can go back and find it.

Large Easel Pad, Corkboard Or White Board

I occasionally use a *large easel pad* when I work. I put my outline on it and fill it in as I write. The large page allows me to put quite a bit more down than a regular notepad. I use this because I am visually oriented when I think of a story. I can scrawl notes all over the large space and refer back to it more easily than if I had twenty smaller sheets of 8.5" by 11" paper.

At the present moment, the easel pad is flat on my desk, with the outline of the end of a book scrawled across in it in numerous notes along with various reminders of editing to be done and phone numbers from calls I received while I was working.

When I was writing with Jenny Crusie, she would have large white boards all over her house. On the boards were every scene in the book broken down into the four acts (hence, four white boards). Each scene was labeled *character versus character* and were color-coded by point-of-view. This gave us an overall visual of the book.

A Lot Of Books

This sounds superfluous, but to be a good writer you have to be well read. Not only that, but as you will see when we get to the research section, often other fiction novels can be good sources for not only facts, but techniques of writing that you will find helpful. Whatever problem you run into, the odds are some writer in the past ran into the same problem—how did they solve it? Then, being the brilliant person you are, you have to figure out a better way.

These are just some of the basic physical tools a writer might want or need. As you will learn from reading this book, there is no right way or wrong way to write a book. Every writer has their own process that has been developed over the course of several manuscripts and in that process are different tools. Whether you can only write on your desktop in your office, or only in your bed in the middle of the night, it is important that you foster those needs with those things that can make the writing come more easily.

Tool 2: The Kernel Idea:
The Alpha & Omega of Your Book

You have to start somewhere.

Have you ever listened to a writer who just recently started a new project? They are practically jumping out of their pants with excitement. Their eyes light up and oddly enough, they break out of that introverted shell and start babbling away about their latest novel.

This is at the core of the Kernel Idea. The spark of inspiration. That one thing that made you believe you could sit alone in a room and write 100,000 words. However, when the writer hits the 50k mark they often forget what excited them in the first place.

The Kernel Idea (The Original Idea)

The kernel idea is the Alpha and the Omega of your book. By that I mean it starts your creative process and it completes it. It's what you begin with and at the end of the manuscript, everything in the book points toward it.

The kernel idea is the foundation of your novel. When I say idea, I don't necessarily mean the theme, although it can be. Or the most important incident, although it can be. But it can also be a setting. It can be a scene. It can be a character.

It's simply the first idea you had that was the seed of your novel. All else can change, but the idea can't. It might be a place; a person;

an event; a moral; whatever. But you did have it before you began writing and you *must* remember it as you write. If you don't, your story and style will suffer terribly. You should be able to tell your idea in one sentence. And repeat it to yourself every morning when you wake up and prior to writing. Knowing it will keep you on track.

For every new book I begin, I write out this one sentence on a word document as the very first writing I do. I print it out and put it where I can constantly see it. The kernel idea is the moment of conception.

Can you clearly state what your book is about in 25 words or less? This is a key, essential ingredient of writing a good book. This idea keeps you focused and on track. It is important to:

Write The Kernel Idea down
Ask yourself: What emotional reaction does it evoke

Good writing and strong characters are the key to great writing and knowing what excited you to write the book in the first place will bleed onto the page. However, if you don't write the idea down, you might forget and get lost along the way.

What Is Your Kernel Idea?
Good news is you had one
Bad news is you probably forgot it
It is usually the first thought you had (the spark of inspiration, the moment of conception)
It is the foundation of your book, the seed

KERNAL IDEA EXERCISE: *Write down the idea behind your current project.*

If you can't do it, then you need to backtrack through your creative process to find it, because you had it at one point. Everything starts from something. While idea is not story (something I will talk about later) idea is the only thing in your manuscript that won't change. Your story can, but your idea won't.

In one of my early novels, the original idea was an action: *What if Special Forces soldiers had to destroy an enemy pipeline?* That's it for *Dragon Sim-13*. Not very elaborate, you say. True. Not exactly a great moral theme. Right. But with that original idea there was a lot I could do and eventually had to do. I had to change the target country after the first draft. But that was all right because I still had the idea. I had to change characters, but that was fine too, because it didn't change my idea. I had to change the reason *why* they were attacking a pipeline, but again, the original idea was the same.

You will have plenty of latitude for story after you come up with your kernel idea; in fact, I sometimes find the finished manuscript turns out to be different from what I had originally envisioned, but one thing is always true: that kernel idea is still there at the end as the Omega.

For my first kernel idea, I made it as simple as possible to enable me to focus on the writing because when I was in the Special Forces my A-Team *had* run a similar mission on a pipeline. Since I had a good idea what would happen in the story, I could concentrate on the actual writing of the novel.

I've sat in graduate literature classes and heard students say, "the author had to have a moral point in mind when they wrote that book." I agree, but sometimes it is not at the forefront of the story. Many authors write simply to tell a story started by that kernel idea, which indeed might be a moral point, but sometimes is a story that they wanted to tell and the theme developed subsequently.

A moral or theme (screenwriters call it intent) always does appear in a book by the time it's done. No matter what conscious expectations or thoughts an author has when they start writing, a lot more appears in the manuscript than they consciously anticipated.

After you have that kernel idea, you should spend a lot of time wrestling with it and consciously uncover your feelings and thoughts about it. I try to look at my main characters and determine what will happen to them emotionally, physically and spiritually as they go through the story. Who are they at the beginning of the story and who are they at the end?

This is an example of being aware of what you are doing. Not all authors have a conscious theme when they write a novel, but experience has taught me that it is better to have your theme in your conscious mind before you start writing. It might not be your kernel idea, but it will definitely affect your characters and story.

The reason it is important to have a theme in mind is because people want to care about what they read and the characters. If there is some moral or emotional relevance to the story they read, they will become more involved in the story and enjoy it more. Even if the reader doesn't consciously see it either.

Some writers balk at the kernel or one-sentence idea. How can you be expected to write the entire essence of your epic novel in one sentence? You are told that every word, every sentence, every paragraph and every scene must have purpose, so how can any writer sum up their work in twenty-five words or less?

It's simple. Your story started with an idea. If you write it down when you think of it, then summarizing your story in one-sentence is that much easier.

One way to work on understanding the Kernel Idea is to take your favorite movie or book and try to figure out the Kernel Idea. This will help you narrow the focus and see how it is the foundation of everything in the story.

Do You Actually Need One Sentence?

I will argue yes, you need one sentence. With that said, how that sentence is developed will depend greatly on your personal creative process. But once you have it down, it becomes a useful tool in all aspects of writing.

If you are a front-loading writer (extensive research/plotter) the Kernel idea might be a natural part of your writing. If you are a back-loading writer (pantser/extensive rewriter) the one-sentence might be a bit harder for you to find. If the idea isn't clear, you might have to spend some time free writing, developing character and getting to know your plot in order to find the one-sentence that will jumpstart your creative process.

Genre can make a difference when it comes to the one-sentence. Thrillers, mysteries, suspense and science fiction lend themselves well to the one-sentence. Sometimes writers will pose a question and that is the center of the one-sentence idea (often starting with What If). Every thing else is built around that key story question (or one sentence idea).

Romance writers and literary writers tend to be focused on character first and need a little time getting to know them before the key story idea forms. The important thing is to write the idea down when it hits you.

Kernel Ideas Can Be Anything
A character
A plot
A setting or scene
An intent
A "What If"

Let's look at some ideas
- **Character:** "A housewife and female assassin must uncover the truth of the men in their lives in order to save their own." *Bodyguard of Lies*
- **Plot:** "What if a Federal agent investigating a murder, finds out it's connected to an illegal CIA operation?" *Chasing The Ghost*
- **Setting or scene:** "An international treaty bans weapons in Antarctica: What if the US put nuclear weapons there and lost track of them?" *Shadow Warriors: The Citadel*
- **Intent/Theme:** "Connection leads to a full life." *Don't Look Down.*
- **"What If":** "What if people going into the Witness Protection Program really disappear?" *The Green Berets: Cut Out*

John Saul at the Maui Writer's Retreat ran a seminar called "What if?" where he had writers put their one sentence up on butcher paper and analyzed it. He made sure every word in the sentence meant something. For example:

What if Mary has to stop a band of terrorists?

How could this be improved? What does Mary mean? Not much. How about 'a housewife'? How about making her a special housewife with an anomaly. *What if an obsessive-compulsive housewife?* However, that term hints at a comedic tone.

Stop a band of terrorists from what? How about 'assassinating the president'? so we understand what's at stake.

This gives us: **What if an obsessive-compulsive housewife has to stop a band of terrorists from assassinating the President?**

That pops, but it makes me wonder how we balance the comedic possibility of the OCD with the high stakes thriller of the assassination? Do you see how your idea raises questions? Both good and bad.

The Importance of Your Kernel Idea

- It starts your creative process
- Remembering it keeps you focused
- It's often the core of the pitch to sell the book

I stress this in my teaching because this one idea is critical to the writing process. It's the one thing I believe every writer should start with, or at the very least, find it before getting too far into the draft.

I also believe every writer should have this on a piece of paper, post-it note, or taped to their computer screen where they can see it at the beginning of every writing session.

Sometimes the kernel idea could even be a way to tell a story, rather than the story itself. Telling the same story from two different perspectives, usually presents two different stories. For example, an idea is "What if a person with limited mental capacity interacts with the world?" The film *A Dangerous Woman* (film works the same way) shows normal, everyday life with the main character being a woman who always tells the truth. You want to talk about someone who is dangerous. Think about it. The film is an excellent portrayal of our society, but the idea was the different perspective. What was *Forrest Gump* about? It had the same basic what if. Wasn't it the main character's perspective that made the story, rather than the actual events?

A different point of view can be a way to tell a story that's already been done in a fresh way. In *Beowulf* the monster had his story to tell and John Gardner did it in *Grendel*. Who was the madwoman in the attic in *Jane Eyre*? She had her story and Jean Rhys told it in *Wide Sargasso Sea*. Jane Smiley put *King Lear* on a present day farm and called it *A Thousand Acres*.

Whenever I watch a film or video I try to figure out what was the original idea the screenwriter had. For example, in the movie *True Romance,* written by Quentin Tarantino, there is a scene at the end where there are four groups of people in a room all pointing guns at each other in a classic Mexican standoff. Rewatching the film, I can see the entire movie driving to that one climactic scene. In an interview, Tarantino said that scene was the kernel idea. He didn't know who the people with the guns were (that's character); where the room was (setting); why they were in the room (motivation); whether it was the beginning, end or middle of the movie (story and plot); what the result of this stand-off would be; etc. etc. He just had this vision to start with.

When I watched the movie *The Matrix*, the scene that stuck out to me was where all those people were plugged and being tapped for their electrical power. I almost sense that was the kernel idea—the screenwriter read or heard that the human body produced X amount of electricity and sat down and thought what he could do with that idea. I think he then came up with the concept of the *Matrix* itself as a follow on.

Kernel Idea And The Pitch
- Sometimes they are the same
- Sometimes they aren't
- But they should be very close
- The Kernel Idea is your tool for your writing
- The Pitch is your tool to sell your writing to someone else

When I teach the A-Team Novel Writer's workshop in a small group, we spend an enormous amount of time on the Kernel Idea. The participants will talk out their ideas, push each other to focus on the excitement and when a writer nails it, it will send a *shiver* up everyone's spine. This is the reason it is the foundation for your writing and for your pitch. It excited you, therefore that idea will excite your readers, whether it be editors and agents or end consumer readers.

Why Is This A Good Idea?
- Why is this idea important?
- What makes it necessary for you to write it?
- What makes a reader want to read it?

There is a big jump between idea and story. I've had great ideas that I couldn't transform into a story. On the other hand, I've taken some not so great ideas and pumped them up with a very good story. The idea is the foundation, once you have that in place, it's time to figure out how you are going to tell the story.

Why Do You Want To Write About This Idea?
- Are you lecturing the reader or entertaining her? You should be entertaining first and foremost
- Is the story about the reader's needs or yours? It's all about the reader

- How well do you know yourself? Yes, back to going to therapy
- Are you demon-slaying, taking revenge, blood-letting? Your first novel should not be the journal you keep in therapy

A critical question I often ask writers at conferences and workshops is: Why did you write this book? I have found that writers tend to get lost among the trees once they enter the forest that a novel is, and they forget why they started the journey in the first place. Something excited you enough at the very beginning, enough that you ended up sitting down and writing thousands upon thousands of words. What was it?

Focusing Your Idea

When you write your one sentence down, check to see what the subject of the sentence is:

1. Character
   - Protagonist or antagonist
   - Plot

Whichever you lead with sends an immediate message to the reader as to which is more important

2. Check to see what the verb is
   - Positive or negative
   - Action or re-action verb

You usually want the verb for the protagonist to be positive, and for the protagonist to eventually act. *Firefly* was a fun series, but it didn't get renewed because there was a fundamental flaw: the protagonist and crew were always escaping and they had no goal other than to not get caught

What If?
- Start your sentence with "What if . . ."

o   Each word must mean something to the reader
o   Don't be a secret keeper
- "What if a thief was using a movie set as a cover for a heist?" *Don't Look Down*
- "What if mankind didn't originate the way we thought?" *Area 51*

Another way to try to figure out what the core of your novel is this: What is the climactic scene? This is when the protagonist and antagonist meet to resolve the primary problem that is the crux of the novel. This is the scene the entire book is driving towards.

Fictional Memoirs
- First novels tend to be blood-lettings and focused on the author, not the reader. Most of us have not led that exciting a life to write a novel about it
- Will anyone else care? Your job as the writer is to make them care

How Is Your Idea Different?
- It isn't: every idea has been done, the difference comes in the transfer to story. Usually through
- Unique character. This is usually the best way. Come up with a fascinating cast of characters, well written, and you could write about anything
- Unique setting. The same idea in a different place, is a different story
- Unique POV. The same idea, told from a different point of view, is a different story. Even the same story told from a different point of view is different
- Unique intent. You twist the same idea so that it has a very different impact on the reader

Where's The Shiver?
What excited you so much that you decided to sit in the dark and write 100,000 words? That's not normal, as already noted. What

excites people you talk to about your book? I know I'm on target with an idea if others pick up my excitement when I discuss it.

Remember, as a writer, you are selling emotion and logic. And Kirk always trumps Spock.

A key to selling your book is being able to communicate this shiver to other people. To get them as excited as you were when you first began writing.

- What excited you?
- What excites the people you tell it to?
- Where's the emotion, the passion?
- What does the reader relate to?
- Can you communicate the shiver?

What's The Payoff?

- How does the idea spark a story that will provide an intent/ theme that provides catharsis?
- How does the idea create a resolution that 'surprises' and sat- isfies the reader?
- Will readers be thinking about, talking about your idea after they finish reading the book?
- Will they find different layers when they re-read it?
- The payoff most likely peaks in the resolution of the story

Study And Find Ideas

- Look for the original idea in every book you read and every movie you watch.
- Usually a sentence or a scene will jump out at you.
- As soon as you finish a book, immediately go back and re- read the opening chapter. The same with watching a movie. If you can, re-watch the opening and now you will find all those things you didn't consciously note the first time. One thing you might pick up in the opening of either the book or movie the second time around is the mirroring of the climac- tic scene. You didn't register it the first time because you

don't yet know what the climactic scene is. We'll discuss this in plot.

Situational And/Or Character Ideas

Every agent I've had has said the same thing to me: a novel can be situation oriented or character oriented. In essence a situation idea relies mostly on plot, while a character idea relies on the people of your story. A situation idea is outward oriented. The best case scenario is to have both a strong plot peopled with strong characters. Ultimately, though, it is most likely that your characters are going to be what sets you apart from everyone else doing the same type of book.

Situation Ideas

- What if people going into the Witness Protection Program really disappear? *The Green Berets: Cut Out*
- What if mankind didn't originate the way anyone thinks? *Area 51*
- What if the force that destroyed Atlantis 10,000 years ago comes back to threaten our present world? *Atlantis*

Character Ideas

- A film producer must save her sister and niece, both physically and emotionally, from a stunt coordinator planning a heist. *Don't Look Down*
- A food critic and a hitman must find out who is trying to kill them and stop the attempts while pulling off a mob wedding. *Agnes and the Hitman*

How is the Kernel Idea the Omega of your book? Because everything you put into that story has to support that one idea. This keeps your book focused and tight. You keep a consistent theme and tone. As you write, and especially once the first draft is done, you have to ask yourself if every scene supports the Kernel Idea. If it doesn't, no matter how brilliantly written that scene is, you must get rid of it.

Idea Is Not Story

Every idea has been done.

There is a very big difference between the idea and the story. I've had great ideas that I couldn't transform into a story. On the other hand, I've taken some not so great ideas and pumped them up with a very good story.

The original idea is the foundation. It's that one sentence beginning. Then you have to figure out how you are going to tell that idea. That's the story. It's the building that goes on top of the foundation.

The difference between idea and story is one reason I don't get very hyper about sharing my ideas with others. I believe two people can have the exact same idea but they will come up with two very different stories.

An idea is usually an abstract. I have found that many fledgling novelists start with the abstract, then got bogged down trying to take that into something concrete (black and white on paper). This is why I beat to death being able to state your idea in one sentence and then writing it down. This makes it real. It makes the distance from idea to story less of a chasm. Even just thinking your original idea is not good enough. You have to state it out loud and write it down on paper. I always find putting thoughts down on paper forces me to focus and I find that this great idea I had in my head suddenly becomes much more difficult to state clearly.

It is a big jump from idea to story. Story includes characters, setting, point of view, pace, intent, etc. etc. Story has to answer all the questions that come to mind the second you tell someone your idea. *Story answers: Who? What? Where? When? How? It also answers the Why of your intent.*

Ambiguity is *not* good in most novels. You have to be a damn good novelist to take your reader along on a vague ride. There are courses dedicated to taking apart and analyzing what exactly did James Joyce mean in his books, but it is not likely they're going to start a course next week on *you* and your book to analyze it. Several authors who teach at universities have really impressed upon me this big problem they have with literature students who think being vague and ambiguous is a good thing when they write. Many times being ambiguous is more a sign of the writer not knowing exactly what they want to say in the first place.

Watch the movie, *The Player*. Watch the writers try to pitch their concept to the character Tim Robbins plays. His line to them all is: "Tell it in 25 words or less." As a novelist pitching to an agent or editor you get at most one paragraph to "hook" them, usually only one sentence. If you can't do it, you've got a problem.

I was watching *Biography* on TV last night and they were covering Clint Eastwood. He would talk about one movie or another and say, "The thing I liked about this screenplay was . . ." And he would sum it up in a sentence or two. He didn't go on and on saying, "boy I really liked the great scene on page 28, and the twist on page 43, and . . ." I find many writers get too caught up in the minutiae of their story and lose sight of the big picture. He bought the screenplay for *Unforgiven* based simply on this pitch: "It's the anti-western." For someone like Clint Eastwood, who'd made so many westerns, the idea of doing the antithesis was intriguing and drew him in.

What do you like about your proposed book? What will draw the reader in?

Another of my favorite lines to go from idea to story is: "Take it one step further." After you "what if", play the one step further game. You'll be surprised where it can take you. What if things aren't as they appear? When you are first starting out don't use this very much, but as you get more proficient at writing, it helps you develop more complex and interesting plots. It allows you to add layers to your story.

I cannot overemphasize the need to be able to have that idea in your mind at all times and to be able to state it in one sentence. It will prevent you from making many of the common errors in manuscripts.

If you cannot tell someone quickly and concisely what your story is, you're going to lose your way when you try to write it. Try talking your story out with someone who knows nothing about it. If you can't succinctly explain it to another person, you are going to have difficulty writing it. If you keep getting stuck halfway through a manuscript, often it's because you forget the idea and have lost the kernel of your book. Writing that idea down and posting it where you can see it every day will really help you stay on track.

Another thing to remember is that almost everything has been done before. The secret is to do it somewhat differently. Many best-selling authors are writers who have *launched* a genre. There was horror before Stephen King but he took it to another level. He admits, for example, that *The Stand*, was inspired by the idea of an earlier book, *Earth Abides*, but King took the idea to a higher level.

Do not write for the *market*. Because you really don't know what the market is going to be in the two and a half to three years it will take you to get traditionally published (if that is the path you choose). The bottom line is to write what you feel you need to. But remember, if you want to sell it, that you need to write it so other people will want to read it.

The kernel idea is also critical when it comes to marketing your manuscript. Guess what the opening line of your query letter is going to be? Guess what is probably the only thing an agent or editor is going to read? Guess what you're going to use in press releases and other promotional material as your opening line?

I know you may think this is terribly unfair. You may feel that taking four hundred pages of brilliant manuscript and trying to sell it on the basis of just a sentence or two is a travesty, but here is something to consider—how do you buy a book?

Most people buy because they know the author and like reading him or her. But if you're a new writer, then you don't have this option. So how do you buy a book from an author you never heard of? Do you stand in the bookstore, read the entire book, then go and pay for it?

Go to your local bookstore or even better, local supermarket. Stand near the paperback racks. Watch how long each person peruses the books on the shelves. How many seconds do they give to each book? Then, when they pick a book up, how long do they spend looking at it? When people look for books online, how much time do they spend on a book's page before moving on?

Why should it be any different for agents and editors?

Story Is
- Who (characters)
- What (plot)
- Where & When (setting)
- Why? (intent)
- Idea can't change, story can
- So, how are you going to do it differently?

Theme and Intent

Theme and intent can be interchangeable. Intent is a term I've stolen from screenwriters. It took me almost ten years of writing and fifteen manuscripts to realize the critical importance of having an intent to my stories, beyond simply being entertaining and having that intent in my conscious mind.

Some in the business of screenwriting say you should be able to state your intent in three words.
- Love conquers all
- Honesty defeats greed
- Honor versus loyalty

There are others who say you need to be able to state it in one word:
- Relationships
- Honesty
- Faith
- Fathers

What Is My Intent?

What do you want readers to walk away with emotionally when they finish reading your story? This is a question many authors don't ask themselves and it's one of the most important questions because it's the readers whom you need to keep coming back for more. When you consider intent, consider your readers first.

Filmmakers have to think about what they want the viewer to feel when they walk out of the theater. This is one reason there are so few negative endings in films. That's not to say you can't have a dark ending. It's more to point out that you need to be aware of the effect of a dark ending.

I've seen some excellent films where the ending was dark and bleak—and often most realistic—but most of those films were not box office blockbusters. The original screenplay for *Pretty Woman* was called *Five Thousand Dollars*. And the Richard Gere character drives away at the end. Realistic, yes. Would it have succeeded as much as the rewrite?

I'm not saying you have to have happy endings and make your reader happy. I'm saying you have to know what feeling you want the reader to experience and make sure you deliver. Larry McMurtry is a master writer and most of his stories have rather bleak endings.

I think that the more negative the intent, the better you have to be as a writer to keep the reader involved. To take readers on a dark and relatively unhappy journey, you have to be very good to keep them in the boat.

Intent

- What do you feel? Why are you writing this book?
- What do you want readers to feel? Do you want them to feel one way or another? Or do you prefer to make it more nebulous where readers could argue about the book's message and intent?
- You always have an intent. Make sure you know it consciously.

- Positive versus negative. Your call, but negative is a harder sell to readers.
- Beware of lecturing. It's called info-dumping. Also, if you take a stand on some matter, realize you run the chance of alienating 50% of your readers. In some instances this is a good thing as it could bring you attention.
- Resolution--the payoff to the reader. Intent peaks in the last scene in the book.

The more a reader feels about a book, the more he will get into it. Feeling comes out of the three aspects of a novel:

1. Idea
2. Intent
3. Characters

If you know and, more importantly, have a good *feel* for each of these three before you begin writing, you increase the quality of your work. We will talk more about character when we get to **TOOL 5: *People the World.***

Unity

Unity is tightening down the story, but it's a good idea to have a basic understanding of unity when you begin writing because unity revolves around emotion. What is the feel of the book? What do you want readers to walk away with? And that goes hand in hand with *Intent.* The key with unity is to get it our of your subconscious and into your conscious and then deliberately line up all the elements of the story to support those things.

The things in your story that make up the spine of the book must all relate to each other for the book to have UNITY, a sense of wholeness. That spine then reflects the Kernel Idea or theme of the book. See how it all comes back to the Kernel Idea?

Motifs & Symbols

Motifs and symbols can help create unity in your book. While they won't be at the forefront of your mind when you begin writing, it is important to pull them from your subconscious and become aware of them so you can use them effectively in your writing.

Ask yourselves what could be the motifs in your book, the repeating images, sounds, words, phrases, events, etc. that build a pattern in the reader's mind? Sometimes your Kernel Idea, your intent and theme, will lend itself to these patterns. But if you're not looking for them, you might miss a great opportunity to connect on a deep emotional level.

Are there any things in your book that might become motifs if you repeated them? They must be repeated at least three times in order to sink into the readers mind.

- What are your symbols, the concrete representations of abstract ideas? This is where show, don't tell, comes in. You use objects to represent the emotions and ideas you want the reader to experience.

- Do your motifs or symbols shift to reinforce plot and character arcs? The same object can be used differently or treated differently so the reader can pick up the arcs in character and plot.

- Why did you choose the opening image in your book? In movies, the first 'shot' often sets the tone. What's the first thing you see on-screen? I always show the opening shot of *Patton* in my workshops and people immediately know what movie it is when they see that huge American flag at the back of the stage. What is your book's opening shot?

- Why did you choose the motifs and symbols you used? Everything in your book serves a purpose. Your subconscious will sometimes insert things into your book that don't seem to do much. At first. That's why you don't edit them out too soon. Leave them. Because those things could end up being critical later on and used another way.

Tone

What tone do I want to achieve in my story?

This is a question not many people think about. For my book *Body-guard of Lies*, one of the few comments my agent came back with was that the tone of the book was inconsistent. He didn't say where, he just said it was. As the author, it was my job to figure out where and why.

What I found was that in my dark, fast-paced thriller, I had a scene that was slow and lighthearted. There's nothing wrong with changing up the pace of a story. In fact, you need to or you will numb the reader out. The problem here was that the change was so abrupt it jarred the reader. You've all read books or watched movies that put you in a certain mood, then suddenly shifted tone, jarring you out of the story. Once in while this actually works as a technique, but only if done for a specific purpose and consciously.

Tone is tied to theme and intent. The tone should support your intent. Think like a film director: how will you light your sets? Will you have a lot of darkness and rain? Or sunshine? Will you put a filter over the camera lens?

Conflict: The Fuel Of Your Story

The Kernel Idea starts your creative process. Conflict is the fuel that keeps your story going. Conflict reveals your characters' true natures and draws the reader closer. It gives the reader a reason to keep turning the page. Without conflict, your idea cannot be translated into story.

Every scene in your book must have conflict. Earlier I mentioned how Jennifer Crusie labeled every scene in our first collaboration by *Character A* vs. *Character B*. Without the versus, there is no conflict. This is an easy way to check every one of your scenes.

Conflict keeps a story going and reveals much about your characters. Conflict is the gap between expectation and the actual result. There are 3 levels of conflict for your characters:

- *inner* (inside the character). In many cases inner conflict occurs when a person has a disagreement between values he or she holds to be important. By adjusting a character's circumstances, you can develop internal conflict.
- personal (between characters)
- universal/societal (characters versus fate/God/the system)

You have to consider what your main character faces on each of these levels.

There are five major sources of conflict for people (although you can probably come up with more):

- Money
- Sex
- Family
- Religion
- Politics

Keep these sources of conflict in mind when developing your characters.

Remember all characters have an agenda/goals they want to achieve. That gives them a driving force, even if it is a passive or negative one. Characters can pursue their goals aggressively or subtly. Or they could not pursue their goals, which also says something about them.

What is Conflict?
- A serious disagreement or argument
- A prolonged armed struggle
- An incompatibility between two opinions, principles or interests
- (v) be incompatible or at variance, clash

The Basic Story Dynamic Is:
- The Protagonist (the character who owns the story) struggles with . . .

- The Antagonist (the character who if removed will cause the conflict and story to collapse)...
- Because both must achieve their concrete, specific . . .
- Goals (the external things they are each trying desperately to get, not necessarily the same thing)

The Protagonist

- Must be someone the reader wants to identify and spend time with: smart, funny, kind, skilled, interesting, *different*
- Must seem real; flawed, layered, have a *blind spot*
- Must have a unique voice
- Must be in trouble, undeserved if possible, but *usually* not random
- Must be introduced as soon as possible, first is preferred
- Must have a strong, believable motivation for pursuing her external and specific goal
- We often empathize with a reluctant protagonist
- We must see the spark of redemption in a negative protagonist very quickly
- The protagonist's blind spot can be the fatal flaw, but at least brings about the moment of crisis
- The protagonist, as she is at the beginning of the book, would fail if thrust into the climactic scene

CONFLICT EXERCISE: *What does your protagonist want most?*

The Protagonist

- Drives the story
- You have one for one main story line
- Does not have to be the hero/heroine or even good
- If she fails, what is the result (stakes)
- Is the person on stage in the climactic scene, defeating the ...

The Antagonist
- Must be someone the reader respects (fears): smart, funny, kind, skilled, interesting, *different*
- Must seem real; flawed, layered, have a *blind spot*
- Must have a unique voice
- Must be in trouble
- Must be introduced as soon as possible, even if by proxy
- Must have strong, believable motivation for pursuing her external and specific goal

CONFLICT EXERCISE: *What does your antagonist want most?*

The Antagonist
- You have one
- Drives the plot initially
- You must do the antagonist's plan and it should be very good
- If removed, the plot collapses
- Should be a single person so the conflict is personal
- Is the person on stage in the climactic scene, fighting the protagonist because . . .

Their Goals Conflict
- The reader must believe both will lose everything if they don't defeat the other
- Their goals are difficult to achieve because of external barriers, primarily each other
- Their goals are layered, usually in three ways . . .

Goal Layers
- **External:** The concrete object or event the character needs
- **Internal:** The identity/value the character is trying to achieve via pursuing the external goal

- **Relationship/communal:** The connections the character wants to gain or destroy while in pursuit of the external goal
- People want to achieve their goals because of their . . .

Motivation

- The reason your character needs his or her goal
- Everyone has an agenda
- Every character has a primary motivator; Frankl's *One Thing*
- Some motivations stem from key events in a character's life

More On Motivation

- The reader must believe that your characters believe all will be lost if they don't achieve their goal.
- Motivations, like goals, come in layers that are peeled away as the story escalates in conflict and the character is under more and more pressure.
- The motivational layers are all present in the beginning of the story, but the character is often not conscious of the layers.
- Thus the motivation and goals shift as the story goes on and we peel away layers...

Layers

- What do you want? In the beginning of *Don't Look Down*, my hero JT Wilder steps off a helicopter. He's a Green Beret on leave, coming to a movie set to advise the lead actor on how to play a Green Beret. Being a guy, what's Wilder consciously thinking? *I'm going to get paid and since there are actresses here, maybe I'll get laid.*
- What do you really want? However, Wilder is pretty much alone in the world. He's left his A-Team and is in a teaching position at Fort Bragg. So on a deeper level he's looking for a relationship.
- No, what do you REALLY need? But he's needs more than just one person. He was part of a team. What he *needs* is a relationship with community.

All these wants and needs were present in Wilder's brain when he got off that chopper. However, the latter two were subconscious. As we hit each turning point in the novel and the pressure grows greater, the surface wants are peeled away until we end up at the need. The last scene of the book is Wilder flying off into the setting sun on a helicopter (mirroring opening scene) except now he's got the relationship, Lucy, sitting next to him and the helicopter is full of people who have grown into a community. Contrast that with the opening scene where he gets off the chopper alone.

CONFLICT EXERCISE: *What is stopping your protagonist from getting what he/she wants most? What is stopping your antagonist from getting what he/she wants most?*

The Central Story Question
- Will the protagonist defeat the antagonist and achieve her goal?
- When the reader asks that question, the story begins.
- When the reader gets the answer, the story is over.

Central Story Question Examples
- *Don't Look Down*: Will Lucy defeat Nash and save herself and her family?
- *Agnes and the Hitman*: Will Agnes defeat Brenda and keep Two Rivers?
- This question leads us to the…

The Conflict Box

The Conflict Box is used to visually diagram your protagonist's and antagonist's goals and conflict. In my writing workshop we spend a lot of time figuring out the one sentence Kernel Idea first. Then we move on to the conflict box as a way of laying out the core conflict and story for the novel.

You can have conflict because

- Protagonist and antagonist want the same thing.
- Protagonist and antagonist want different things, but achieving one goal causes conflict with the other's goal.

The Conflict Box

The core conflict based on goals that brings the protagonist and antagonist into direct opposition in a struggle that neither can walk away from. A key to filling out the conflict box is to look at each box separately and fill them in one by one. The goal box must have a concrete, external goal in it. Don't confuse goal with motivation. The conflict is what's stopping the character from getting that thing.

Conflict Diagram

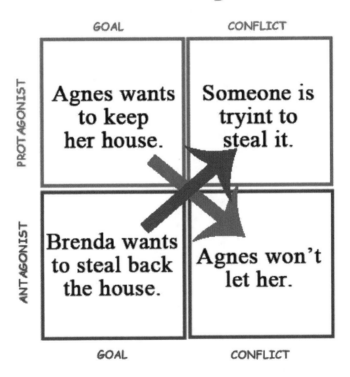

Conflict Box: Same Goal In Agnes And The Hitman

- *Protagonist Goal:* Agnes wants to keep her house, which she bought from Brenda
- *Antagonist Goal:* Brenda wants to steal back the house she just sold to Agnes
- *Protagonist Conflict:* Someone is trying to steal the house from Agnes
- *Antagonist Conflict:* Someone won't let Brenda steal the house

To see if your conflict is inescapable. Draw a line from Agnes' goal to Brenda's Conflict. If Agnes is causing Brenda's conflict, you're halfway there.

Then draw a line from Brenda's goal to Agnes' conflict. If Brenda is causing Agnes' conflict, you have a conflict lock. Not that a house is a concrete object and it is very clear who has it.

The key to the conflict box is one character **must** cause the other character's **conflict.** You have that, you have conflict lock.

Conflict Box: Different Goals In Lost Girls

- *Protagonist Goal:* Gant wants to find out who is kidnapping and killing young girls
- *Antagonist Goal:* The Sniper wants to continue killing and kidnapping the daughters of those he feel betrayed him
- *Protagonist Conflict:* Someone keeps kidnapping and killing young girls
- *Antagonist Conflict:* Someone is trying to stop him kidnapping and killing young girls

Cross the arrows from the two boxes and you have conflict lock.

CONFLICT EXERCISE: *Fill out the conflict box for your book.*

Filling out a conflict box accomplishes a lot of key things. Here's what I discovered in my writing workshop:

- People can't correctly identify who the protagonist and/or antagonist is.
- People can't find the concrete object each character wants. They put motivation in the box. We can't see motivation (we'll cover this in more detail under character). Whatever is in that box is something the reader can see and we know when they either have achieved it or failed in achieving it.
- The conflict must be something standing in the way of the character trying to achieve their goal.

Tool 3: Preparation

What To Write

Mark Twain said, "Write what you know." I have some addendums to that "Write what you want to know."

Elizabeth George writes best-selling mysteries based in England and she lived in California. I write about myths and legends because they interest me and I'm willing to do the research to learn more. I believe that if I can find material that interests me, it should interest some readers.

Write what you are passionate about. You should care greatly about the people and story. Writing about something you care about very deeply has the advantage of adding passion to your prose. It also has the disadvantage that some writers can't separate themselves enough from what they write to adequately judge its content or style. I've watched writers waste *years* on the same manuscript, trying to polish the editing, doing rewrites on various subplots, etc. when they were not willing to accept a fundamental problem with their story: the basic idea wasn't that interesting.

I've seen many writers become too emotionally attached to bad ideas. Remember I mentioned earlier that open-mindedness is a very important trait for writers. Too many writers get tunnel vision and fail to objectively evaluate their own work in terms of someone who has no emotional attachment and is seeing it for the first time. Just because you feel something, that doesn't mean you can get the reader to feel the same thing.

Usually your background will dictate what your story is about. That's not to say that since you haven't ever gone into space that you can't write science fiction, but it does mean that you know something about the physics of space flight if that's going to be in your manuscript. Think about when you read the book jacket for a writer you never heard of. If they've written a thriller that's set in Antarctica and in the bio it says they spent three years studying ice formations in Antarctica you're going to give the author more credit.

I think it's even easier than that: you will most likely write whatever it is you enjoy reading. The best preparation for becoming a writer of mysteries is to have read a lot of mysteries.

Some words of advice here: start with something simple. Don't try to write the Great American Novel on your first try. I'm constantly learning more about writing and am polishing my skills every time I write and it's nice to be able to learn and make a buck at it too. As I learn more, I can write more difficult plots and characters.

And now some words of caution. I've said you should write what you know and you should keep it as simple as possible, but be careful. A common problem with new writers is thinking that *their* life story will be extremely interesting to the reading world, the fictional memoir I discussed earlier. This is an addition to Mark Twain's saying. There is nothing inherently wrong with writing about yourself, but be realistic about the possibilities of someone else wanting to read it.

There is a problem every writer faces when approaching his or her first manuscript: You are trying to do something new. Most wise people when trying to do something new use the KISS technique— keep it simple. You are trying to juggle two glass balls: the story and the writing. The simpler you make the story, the more attention you can give to the writing.

That sounds rather simplistic, but I've seen many writers get in over their heads by trying to write a very complex first novel and the writing suffers as they wrestle with the story. Most first novelists can do one or the other well, but very few can do both well. Since you must write well, give yourself a break on the story. When I was still unpublished and got hooked up with an agent, his first (and only) comment to me was to simplify the plot of the manuscript he had looked at. I had too much going on and was not a skilled enough writer to keep it all going. I did as he suggested and that book was the first one we sold.

In fact, I've come full circle. I've written a couple of series of books that have done well but are very complicated, with complex story lines involving a large cast of characters and generally rewriting the entire history of mankind. Talk about difficult. I've also written some thrillers that were quite complicated. The next book I write that's not under contract is going to be a very simple idea and story line where I can focus on giving my characters the depth I used to devote to the plot.

One thing to be careful of with your first novel and one of the reasons first novels rarely sell: often the first book a person writes is an expunging of personal demons. Thus the book holds great emotional weight for the writer but it might not do the same for the reader.

Another problem: perfectionism. Some people think that the writing has to be perfect. They spend an inordinate amount of time on editing and rewriting. Sometimes, you just have to accept it's either good enough, or that the horse is dead and can't be brought back to life.

I am going to go on here on my soapbox a little bit longer. I just finished looking at a couple of dozen "novel submissions" for a contest I am judging. I have yet to see one that was not about "love, death, divorce, child abuse, broken hearts, etc. etc." Nobody said, "Hey, I've got a great science fiction story here." Or a horror story. Or a thriller. There's nothing wrong with writing about love, death, etc. but none of the writers were up to the task.

Go to the bookstore. Look around. What is the largest section? From the bookstores I frequent, the answer is: Computers. Second largest? Self-help. Ah—what is self-help about? "Love, death, addiction, child abuse, broken hearts, etc. etc." And last I checked it is non-fiction.

Remember why people read fiction: most of the time we read to escape "death, abuse, addiction, broken hearts, etc. etc." We read primarily to be entertained. Yet, here are all these aspiring writers trying to write what I call The Great American Novel. How many of these types of books are on the bookshelves? Maybe 10 to 20 percent of the hardcover new releases. Less than 10% of the paperback original releases. You figure it out.

I believe that this is the number one problem most new novelists have: they pick very difficult subject matter for their story. The craft of writing is hard enough. The more difficult the topic is, the better the writing has to be.

The bottom line is that you need to have an original thought/idea that will spark you and others.

Writing For The Market

What's hot? I get asked that a lot. And my reply is, "Who cares?" First, you have to write your passion, not someone else's, or just to please the market. Also, in traditional publishing it's around three years from idea to bookstore. What's hot now, might not be hot in three years.

Don't try to ride the latest wave. This is an area where there is a large degree of luck. You might be fortunate and have written a book about Seal Team 6 and just before scheduled publication, ST-6 shoots Bin Laden. Bad for him, good for your book.

The key question is: will anyone else care about what I've written? And the answer is that it's your job as the writer to do such a good job, that you make them care. Writing about something you don't care about will show up in the material.

GENRE

Where Does Your Book Fit And What Does It Mean To Be Literary?

Genre is key to finding readers and marketing. Most novels are going to fit into not only a genre, but a sub-genre inside of it, that makes the book even more niche. Niche is good in the current market. The problem for many writers is they don't understand what genre their book is. They'll say something like: "I've written a mystery thriller." You can have mystery in your thriller or thrills in your mystery, but it's one or the other primarily.

I define literary writing as writing about real life. Day to day living. The more you write about ordinary life, the more extraordinary your writing must be. People live every day life. To take them into it, and engross them, you must be a superb writer.

If you write about extraordinary events, then the writing does not necessarily need to rise to this same high standard. I'm not saying you can be bad, but I am saying the core of the story can then engross the reader.

A major mistake new novelists make is trying to write the Great American Novel right off the bat before becoming proficient enough at the craft to be an artist.

Decide where your book fits (if it does fit). No one likes hearing it, but there are certain guidelines to follow when writing in specific fields. If you are writing a thriller, then your primary emphasis is on action and the ticking clock that the plot relies on. That's not to say that you shouldn't have good characterization, but you should not emphasize the characters at the expense of slowing down the action. Remember the expectations of the reader: when they bought your book, or picked it up to read, why did they do that? What are they looking for?

As I've said before, the second most important thing an aspiring writer should do (with writing being number one) is read. Read everything you can get your hands on in the field you are trying to write in. Read the authors in your field. Read the good ones. Read the bad ones. Dissect the books and try to find commonalities, then find where some authors were a little different.

Walk into a bookstore and look at how it's laid out (or examine how Amazon breaks out fiction into genres and sub-genres). You have a fiction section; a mystery section; a science fiction section; etc.

etc. You should be intimately familiar with the section that you propose to write in. You should know who the authors are. You should know who the publishers are. You should be a member of the appropriate writer's group, for example, Sisters In Crime for mystery writers. Optimally, you should go to a writer's conference where a writer in your field will be and try to get information first hand. Go to the library and look up copies of Publishers Weekly or sign up for PW Daily and PW Deals for $20 a month and go through the reviews and deals and see what is being published, by who, and what agents represent the various deals.

The RWA publishes statistics on genre book sales, which you should be aware of:

- Romance: 55.9% of all fiction sold in North America.
- Mystery/Detective/Suspense: 28.1%
- Science Fiction/Fantasy: 7.2%
- That only leaves 8.8% for everything else.

I am not saying that you have to fit into a genre. I am simply saying that most writers do. If you look at the recent history of publishing, there are certain names that stick out: King, Clancy, Crichton, Grisham, etc. What each of these have in common is that they basically "launched" a new genre. That's not to say that there weren't horror books before Stephen King, but it is to say that somehow King did something a little different and broke open the field. In the same manner, Tom Clancy is the leader of the pack in military techno-thrillers.

Pretty much everything has been done before. The secret is to do it better and/or do it differently with a new twist.

You really cannot try to beat the market place. The time lag between concept and being in the bookstore for most authors averages around three years. So while lawyer books might be hot this year, don't count on it being hot by the time you get that book done and marketed. *Write what you can write and what you want to write.*

I remind you of genre only to make it easier for you to study what has been done to help you do what you want to. With self-publishing you can do it more quickly, but even then, if it's not a subject you are passionate about, it will show up in the writing.

There are times when you don't want to fit in a genre. One of my publishers didn't want to list my *Area 51* series of books as science fiction because they felt they could reach a broader audience if they label it mainstream. Regardless, Amazon has placed those books in science fiction. Mainstream is what everything that doesn't definitely fit into one of the categories of genre—which are basically: science fiction/fantasy, mystery and romance—goes.

A key thing to remember, also, is that your story does not have to be enjoyed by everyone. If you are writing a romance and you hand it to someone who has never read—nor likes—romance novels, to read and critique, don't expect very good feedback. If one person in ten out of your writer's group says, "Hey, I really liked that." then think about it—ten percent of the selected population liked your story. If ten percent, or even one percent, of the people who enter a bookstore wants to buy it, then you have a bestseller.

Earlier I mentioned that it seems like most aspiring writers (and writing programs) disdain genre and try to write books about "life". But go back to my analogy to being a student of architecture. The reason I always suggest to a new novelist to write a genre novel or two first before moving on to the Great American Novel is because it's like the architecture professor giving his student a set of blueprints and saying: "Here's a rough set of guidelines of buildings like the one you want to build—and all these guidelines worked. Now, use these as a reference and design your own."

Putting a novel together is so difficult that any way you can help yourself in the beginning is useful and, not to beat this to death, but making not only the subject of your novel, but the format, a familiar one will help you. If you read five romance novels a week, then you have "studied" romance writing quite a bit. You know the format. The flow of the book. You even know quite a bit about the business end (you know authors, publishers, and the market.).

I'm not saying write "formula" books. The point, though, is that genre is not only the way publishers look at books and categorize them, it is also the way readers categorize books.

Another helpful aspect of understanding what genre you are writing in, is that there are writers groups for most genres. Sisters In Crime comes to mind. There are science fiction groups, mystery groups, and fantasy groups. There are also conventions and workshops designed specifically for those areas, such as Boucheron. The Romance Writers Association, RWA, is an extremely professional and well-run group.

Regardless of genre, your goal should be to write the best possible book you can both in terms of plot and characterization.

The Literary Genre

I have added this after attending a writers' retreat where I read one of the participant's manuscript. It was about a woman and the way her life changed in response to events in it and her own growing maturity as a person. It made me reevaluate some of the things I've taught and written in this book. My focus used to be on action driven stories because that is what I did. It is what I did because it is what I was capable of doing. If I were capable of writing *War and Peace, The Sequel* I suppose I would do that, but I'm not. Yet.

Many writers want to write about people, not specifically action. There's nothing wrong with that. I have perceived though, that there are some things to keep in mind in a character oriented book and I will touch on what little I have learned and experienced.

In a character oriented book you should treat your characters like you would subplots in an action book. For example, don't have a character in chapter 3 if you don't develop and use that character by the end of the novel. To abuse the Chekov quote I used earlier, don't have a character in your story unless that character impacts the main plot by the end. Just as all subplots must be kept tight to the main plot, all your characters must be tight to the main story, which is your main character's development.

Each character must be real and have his or her own agenda, just like each person in real life has his own agenda, even if it isn't a conscious one. The characters must also be consistent. Connecting all the characters should be an over-arcing theme.

Also realize that perhaps the greatest flaw most people have is their lack of awareness of *themselves*, never mind others. True characters are not walking around self-actualized on Maslow's hierarchy. Many times they are walking around ignorant of their own agenda. Sometimes authors are also ignorant of their own agenda, specifically why they are trying to write a novel.

I have also found that character oriented books often need to be cut down much more than action oriented books. There is a tendency to wander a bit, because people's lives tend to wander a bit. Now, there are some authors whose style is so good that you like that wandering—say, a Larry McMurty or Pat Conroy. But for most, less is better.

Some authors come to mind for these types of books: Lisa Alther, Anne Tyler, Richard Russo, Jane Smiley, Clyde Edgerton and many more. If you want to write like these people, you should read everything you can that they write. You should study the craft of writing, of putting words into sentences into paragraphs.

One thing for sure: The quality of writing in a character oriented book must be higher because it must evoke emotion in the reader, not just intellectual interest.

The Reader

The One Who Pays Your Salary
I have to remind myself that I spend many months full-time writing something that will be read by others in several hours. I also have to remember what mindset the reader approaches my novels with. I have to both tell a story interesting enough to keep the reader's

attention (intellect) and tell it in a manner that the reader feels connected to the characters (emotion). As a writer, you need to be aware of these things.

Don't forget what the reader knows. If the reader knows something that a character in your story doesn't, it makes the story harder to write and you must be more skillful. You have to do this sometimes, but be very careful to not confuse or bore your reader. Don't go 10 pages with your character agonizing over who killed Aunt Bess if the reader was shown Uncle John strangling Aunt Bess in chapter two, something your character obviously wasn't privy to.

I find this to be a big problem that many new writers have, and it comes about because of point of view. If the writer has a scene that reveals who the bad guy is in chapter 2, but the protagonist doesn't know who the bad guy is until chapter 14, those twelve chapters in between, wherever the protagonist is trying to discover who the bad guy is, are a real turn-off to the reader.

In the same manner if you have an ensemble cast of characters traveling all over the world, you run into the problem of what we used to call in the army *dissemination of information*. The reader knows all of what all the characters know, but the characters don't know what each other knows. I used to have scenes where my characters literally all sat around a conference table and exchanged information—at least that is until an editor pointed out to me how boring those scenes were to the reader.

Don't underestimate the reader. If they can read, they have at least a base level of education. Don't beat the reader to death to make a point. Most writers err on the side of overkill; although just as dangerous a trait is being so subtle the reader misses it. Usually, though, the difference between a book and a movie is that the reader can go back three pages and reread something to check it. Also remember most people read every word and aren't likely to miss what you write. They may miss the *significance* of what you've written (which is useful in building suspense and having neat twists) but usually when the reader gets to the end and learns what really happened (if it's well written) they suddenly see the significance of things they didn't pay much attention to. Thus mention Uncle John maybe only once, instead of twenty times. Yeah, he was mentioned and the especially astute reader may pick up your clue, but even the most obtuse will get it if you rant on about Uncle John's massive forearms and great hand strength in chapter 10. Then happen to mention several times how he likes to pop the heads off chickens in chapter 12 and how he used to set fires and torture small animals as a kid in chapter 14—get the point? Or do I have to beat you to death with it?

When remembering your reader, do not sell your reader short. Give the reader credit for putting some brain effort into the book. There is a tendency for beginning writers to either beat a reader to death with a point that they feel is important (i.e. repeating it several times on the same page) or being too subtle because the writer knows what's going on but forgets that the reader doesn't.

In the first case, overuse of language can be a problem. If a character is upset and you basically say that once, to use very strong adjectives or adverbs further on, to further emphasize the character's state of mind can actually detract. It is almost like using dialogue poorly. Let the actions, not the adjectives and adverbs speak.

An Example Of This Common Mistake

"Listen you idiot," Buffalo Bill angrily screamed at the quivering boy. *"You've really made me mad now,"* he furiously added as he pounded the stock of his rifle into the dead buffalo's already smashed skull.

Think Buffalo Bill is angry? Uh-huh.

Also don't lecture the reader. Sometimes you will write something you feel very strongly about, but really adds little to the story. Cutting something out of your manuscript is one of the most painful things to do but one of the most necessary. I had a thirty-page chapter in my second novel that I was very proud of. It was a Special Forces brief-back that went into superb detail on the upcoming mission. Unfortunately, it slowed down the action of the book and I made the decision to cut it down extensively and Chapter Six went from thirty pages to five in the final version. Concentrate on the overall story, not parts of the story.

I've even heard someone say that you should cut out the part of the manuscript that you absolutely love the most because your emotion is clouding your judgment. There is a certain degree of validity to taking a hard look at the parts in your story that you feel most strongly about. It might even be just a sentence that strikes you each time you read it, jarring you out of the story, or even a word. Be prepared to cut.

Another mistake is too much foreshadowing. I found that I tended to *set up* plot points a bit too much instead of allowing them to occur naturally. I mention elsewhere Chekov's rule of not having a gun in Act One unless you fire it by the end of Act Three, but be careful not to mention the gun too much or the reader loses all suspense.

The most important thing you have to remember about the reader though is that you have to interest him. You have to get him involved with your story. You can never assume you interest the reader. You have to focus on making sure you do that on every page.

Even now, when I publish a book, I step back from it and look at it on the racks in the bookstore. I ask myself why should someone who has never heard of me pick up that book and even look at the back cover, never mind buy it? What makes my book stand out?

That leads me to this brilliant observation I made after publishing 10 books and writing 15 manuscripts: **Title is important.**

I look at the titles for my first eight books now and I cringe. There is little in the title of any of those books to interest the reader. So then why should they pick up and even check to see what it's about? Do that yourself. Go to the bookstore and just scan. Besides the cover art (if the book is fortunate not to be spine out), what do you notice?

The title. And which ones catch your interest? It is something very important to think about and consider.

Mary Higgins Clark says title should invite you into the book. Many authors come up with a title that only makes sense if you read the book; i.e. the title comes out of the book. But that's backwards logic. Because no one is going to read the book unless the title draws them in. I recommend spending a considerable amount of time thinking about your title. I believe it is the only marketing device the writer has control of.

Title should work one of two ways: It should entice the reader by giving a clear idea what the book is about, i.e. *Clear and Present Danger* signals the book is a thriller. Or be a juxtaposition of two words that don't belong together and therefore intrigue: *Lovely Bones*.

The bottom line is that the reader is the most important factor in the entire publishing arc that goes from writer, through agent, to editor, to publisher, to bookseller, to bookstores, to reader. And in today's world it goes almost directly from writer to reader.

The Concept of Process

Process is how you write. Plot? Character? Plot? Pantser? In an office? At the beach? At the kitchen table? Outline? Synopsis? Process is everything you do from the light bulb moment (Kernel Idea) that made you think you could sit alone and write a hundred thousand words, to the moment you say the manuscript is ready for the world to see.

The key to process is to have a starting point and basic understanding of how you work as a writer. We spend a fair amount of time in my *Write It Forward* program discussing who we are as individuals and how that affects our daily routine. Understanding self will help to understand your writing process on a conscious level.

The writing process is as unique as every individual. It is also as unique as every book. I have not written a single book exactly the same since I started. Each time I sit down to write, I'm learning about myself. I'm trying to correct mistakes I've made in past manuscripts and hoping not to make new ones. I'm keenly aware of my shortcomings as a writer and focusing on those aspects while not relying too heavily on those strengths that carried me through the last book.

Much of what happens to us as writers isn't on the conscious plane. We have to look for and develop our writing rituals and habits and bring what we do in our subconscious to our conscious mind. It's hard to know what your process is the first time you write a book. However, you can begin to map your process out the first time you open a word document and start typing.

Process is a way of outlining your creativity. Here are some questions to help you figure out how you write a novel.

- Do you start with character, plot or place?
- Is your focus on the protagonist or the antagonist?
- Do you develop characters beforehand or do they develop as you write?
- Do your settings have to be real places or do you invent them?
- If you're a detail person, how do you see the big picture of the novel?
- If you're a big picture person, how do you keep track of the details of your story?
- Do you write steadily, a certain amount each day?
- Or do you burst write, knocking out large sections, then having to recuperate for several days?

You need to study your procedure for writing, both day to day, and overall, in order to refine your process. Most successful authors I know are constantly working on their process and are very conscious of what they are doing with their writing. It's not this vague, artistic flow for most. It's a very regimented and disciplined process.

The Beatles did a song about being a writer with the basic philosophy that it's an easy road to fame and fortune. It's a profession where anyone with access to paper and ink thinks they can join the ranks. The longer I do this, though, the more I believe that it is very important to learn the basic craft of writing a novel before exercising one's genius. If you talk to coaches of teams, they always stress learning the fundamentals first, and I feel the same way about writing. Too often, inexperienced writers jump deeply into too complicated a story before having the tools in order to set up the basic structure to make that leap.

I just spent several days looking through manuscript submissions and saw so many basic mistakes it made me wonder if the writers even read books, never mind had studied writing. It's like the architect I mentioned earlier. Before one can build a spectacular bridge, it helps if one has at least looked at a couple of simple bridges to gain the experience.

Here's a checklist of things that I constantly find in manuscripts. I address each of them in the various chapters that follow, but I want to list these up front to gain some focus:

1. ***Hooking the reader.*** Many writers spend too much time giving background information, introducing various characters, etc. before they introduce...
   - The plot, and
   - The main character
2. ***Dialogue tags.*** The words inside the quotation marks have to get across to the reader the necessary information and emotion. Trying to make up for the lack in written dialogue by overusing eccentric dialogue tags is very common and very jarring.
3. ***Repetition.*** Using the same words over and over again, or same phrases, is very jarring to the reader.
4. ***Time sense and pacing of the story.*** I call this the remote control effect. A story should flow in some sort of logical time

sequence. Too often stories fast-forward, then rewind to a flashback or memory, jumps forward, slow down, speed up, etc. etc. until the reader's head is spinning.

5. ***Setting the scene.*** Often I begin reading a scene/chapter and am totally lost for several pages as to where this action is occurring, who is in the scene, when this scene is in relation to the last scene.

6. ***Characters talking to themselves.*** This is a weak technique to give expository information or thoughts to the reader. What do you think of someone who wanders around talking to himself or herself all the time? Also, this technique used in conjunction with an actual conversation can be very confusing because the reader will not be sure which dialogue is directed at the other participant in the conversation and which is directed back at the speaker.

7. ***Misuse of pronouns.*** If you have two men in the room and use the phrase *"Blah, blah, blah," he said.* It had better be very clear which he you are referring to. The technical definition of a pronoun is: *one of a class of words that function as substitutes for noun or noun phrases and denote persons or things asked for, previously specified or understood from the context.* It needs to be very clear whom your pronoun refers to. Don't confuse the reader.

8. ***The difference between a memory and a flashback.*** This is also covered elsewhere.

9. ***Slipping into second person point of view.*** Any time you address the reader as I am now addressing you, then you are into second person POV.

Where Most People Go Wrong

After looking at manuscripts and concepts for years, I made a list of what I considered the top five problems. Initially, the first several years, I focused on perspective as the major problem. As time went on though, and I learned more about writing, I changed that opinion. If a manuscript's major problem is point of view, then at least the writer got out of the starting gate. To my dismay I have found that many writers never make it out of the starting gate. I then decided that not having a good idea was the major problem with most manuscripts. Years after making that decision, I revised my list once more and what you have below has been updated several times.

So my ranking of problems is more of a creative flow ranking rather than a percentage.

Characters

You engage the reader on the emotional and intellectual levels. Good characters can overcome everything else because they touch the reader emotionally which is the most important aspect of a novel. When Anne Tyler wrote *Breathing Lessons* the basic story was two people driving from Baltimore to Pennsylvania for a funeral and then back home. Not the world's most startling idea or story. But the characters were done so well the book is a great read. For me, this was one of the greatest lessons I've had to learn over the years: people are more interested in people than anything else.

I just read a book about the battle of Thermopylae that sold quite well. What I realized reading it was that the aspect of the book that intrigued readers was not so much the battle, but the Spartans—readers were fascinated to learn how men could become soldiers that would stand and die to the last man in that mountain pass in Greece.

Why is Stephen King the #1 horror writer? There are other writers out there who do horror as well as he does. But he does great characters that draw the reader into the story, and then when the horror strikes, it has more of an impact because of that emotional involvement.

If you want to see a great example of introducing characters and engaging readers with them, read the first ten pages of *Lonesome Dove*. Larry McMurtry introduces Call, Gus, Newt, Jake Spoon, Deets and several other characters in such a way that you immediately have a feel for them.

The Idea

You've got to have a good idea to start with. Too many manuscripts are written about something that really won't interest anyone enough to plunk down hard cash to read it.

I beat to death earlier, and will later, the ability to state your idea succinctly. After you master that, find out if it works as a hook. When you look at a complete stranger on the bus going to work and say: "I read a book the other day about ----(insert your idea)." How do they react? Are they interested? Do they call the police and have you carted off? Or, most likely, do they stare at you blankly without interest?

The idea is the thing that will intrigue readers more on the intellectual side of the house. You put good characters together with a great idea and the sky is the limit.

Story

If a manuscript has an intriguing original idea and good characters, then the next issue is: is the story interesting? How many times have you picked up a book or heard about a movie that sounded interesting and then got turned off by the manner in which the story was told?

My first novel published, *Eyes Of The Hammer*, was about US military forces going to South America and attacking drug labs. Tom Clancy came out with *Clear and Present Danger* at the same time. The original ideas in the two were similar. But the way in which we told the story was quite different. He told it from the top looking down, while mine was from the bottom looking up. I focused on the Special Forces team, which I knew well, while he took a more global view.

The story is a major stumbling block. I can pitch you ten very good ideas at any moment. But each of those ten would take me quite a while to come up with a good supporting story. In fact, in eight of the ten, I probably would not be able to come up with a good story.

I spend a lot of time working on story after I have an idea. I war game various stories with my partner and we discuss them. Ultimately, and you are going to cringe to hear this, I don't proceed with a storyline until it *feels* right. This is part of the artistic craft in writing, but a pretty realistic one. You have to feel comfortable that you can write your story and that it is interesting not only to the reader, but also to you the writer.

Perspective/Point of View

I have a whole section dedicated to this style problem. But I have found that when a person has trouble writing action scenes the first thing I look for is to see if the author is handling perspective well. When dialogue drags, I check. As a matter of fact, when there is any style problem, the first thing I look at is the perspective the story is being told in, rather like you would check to see if there was any gas in the tank if a car's battery (the idea) was putting out juice, but the engine wouldn't fire.

Perspective is your voice as a writer.

Timeline Or Pacing Of The Story

This comes up very quickly at times because too many writers don't knock the reader's socks off with their opening two chapters. Most of us aren't a good enough writer to spend a hundred pages slowly drawing the reader in. You have to hook them and hook them fast. I have a chapter on how to start your novel and a chapter on pacing that addresses these problems.

Following The Tools In This Toolkit

You start with your Kernel Idea, which you can state in one sentence and is exciting.

You figure out your protagonist, antagonist, and core conflict (conflict lock).

Remember to stay open-minded to possibilities. So now you . . .

Research: The Story's World and Get the Details You'll Need

There are two types of research: primary and secondary.

Primary research is related to specifics of the story you are going to tell.

Secondary research goes on all the time and should be second nature to a writer—it's called living and being tuned in to the world. You should be observing things around you all the time. You should also be well read. Many times your ideas come out of research in the first place.

I had a demolition's man on my Special Forces team and whenever we went anywhere he was always looking at things around him and figuring out how he would blow them up. Every dam we passed, power line, bridge, etc. he was estimating how many charges it would take and where he would place them. As a writer you should be always thinking like that—how you would write things you see, describe people you observe? How would you show what you observe without telling?

The number one thing a writer must do is write. I would say the number two thing is read. Read for information and read for style. Read for format. Reading books like the type you want to write is probably the best possible research you can do.

Every Book You Read, You Should Be Taking It Apart In Two Ways

- Overall narrative structure
- Scene by scene plot/character development.

When I get stalled writing, I'll turn my seat and look at the wall behind me that is filled with bookcases. I'll look at titles of the books there, remembering the stories, and it will both inspire me and also give me ways around problems I'm facing in my current manuscript. Remember, as a writer, you are not alone if you have books.

Watch Films

Although the medium is different, the dramatic concept is basically the same. Another key to watching film is that a screenwriter must absolutely show not tell. Watch how they get ideas and emotions across strictly through showing. Also, focus on the camera work—the point of view the director chooses to tell the story. Where is the camera location for each shot? When is there a cut? When does the camera move in on a character and move out? Why? How is light used? Shadow? Tone? Colors?

In many cases, research helps you construct the story after you have your initial idea. Research is not just looking outward for information, it's also looking inward. Make sure you know the real reason you are writing the story you've decided to. Whatever you feel about the story is going to bleed out onto the page.

Setting

Research your setting (place & time). There is nothing equal to actually standing in a place and getting the feel for it. I call it 'walking the terrain.'

You can never have enough information. Even while writing I look for more information about the topic I am writing about. All my books have started from the Kernel idea and then the story developed out of the research I did on that idea and related areas.

One question people ask is how factual their stories should be? Where is the line between realistically portraying something and making things up? That's a difficult question to answer. My science fiction books are only science fiction in that I give a different explanation for things that actually exist. It is a fact that there are large statues on Easter Island. The fiction in my *Area*

51 series comes in when I give my own explanation for why those statues were made.

Writing historical fiction, I'd better have my dates correct. And the historical characters in the right place at the right time doing the thing they did. However, no one knows what these people really said in most cases, unless it was specifically recorded, such as Lincoln's Gettysburg Address.

If you are writing a mystery you can't be too far off base with your police procedural information, although the focus should be on character, not technique. One of the most successful detective series of all-time, *Inspector Morse*, didn't rely on forensics or car chases, but rather on the human interaction among the characters.

I think many people are lulled by the inaccuracies portrayed in movies. Books have to be more accurate for several reasons; one is that the average reader is more on the ball than the average moviegoer; second, you can slide something by in a couple of seconds of film but the reader can linger over and reread a paragraph again and again. A reader can also turn back from page 320 to check page 45 where you mentioned the same thing and compare the two.

The Internet

The Internet is useful in gathering information as there is a web page about practically everything. I had a scene in one of my Area 51 books where a character is attacked by piranha while crossing a river in South America. Having personally never been attacked by piranha, I searched the web and found several pages devoted to the creatures.

Another strength of the Internet is networking. There is every possible organization out there with a web site and then there are places like Facebook and Twitter. I'm not getting into those in detail, because there are other books out there for that.

The Internet is a useful way to get in contact with other writers and even agents and editors. I maintain a web site of my own through which people can e-mail me. Be warned though: you should spend the majority of the time on your computer writing, not surfing. I am a firm believer in turning off my wireless while I write. It's off right now.

Old Fashioned Books

Also, I still use books a lot for research. While the Internet can get your specific information it also has flaws. First, you have to have an idea what you're looking for. Second, the Internet often doesn't give you interesting details you can only find in a book. Third, the Internet sometimes can't give you a 'feel' for a topic. Reading U.S. Grant's *Memoirs* and then several biographies about him gave me insight into his character I could have never gotten from finding facts on the Internet.

Some Examples Where Research Using A Book Adds To Story

1. I was writing a book titled *Area 51 The Sphinx*. Therefore I did a lot of research on the Great Sphinx. In a thick tome I was wading my way through there was one sentence that caught my attention. It said that Sir Richard Francis Burton, a man who'd always fascinated me, visited the Great Sphinx in 1855. The opening scene of the novel ended up being this visit. Then, as I researched Burton, I learned that upon his death, his wife burned a manuscript over his body. A large part of the book became a chase in the present day to discover a copy of the manuscript and decrypt the secrets it contained.

2. Years ago, I was wandering the library and saw a book titled: *Japan's Secret War*. I picked it up and was quite intrigued at the author's premise that the Japanese actually developed a working atomic bomb and detonated it in Manchuria in the waning days of World War II. As a fiction writer, this was a premise I could run with and I took it one step further: what if there were a second bomb, and it was taken by submarine to

San Francisco at the end of the war and left at the base of the Golden Gate bridge? I ended up with *Black Ops: The Gate*.

3. I was researching Vikings because one of my *Atlantis* books has half the storyline set in the year 1,000 AD. In one book I read about an interesting character named Corpse-Loddin, whose career was to sail out in the spring and recover the bodies of Vikings who were trapped the previous winter by ice and killed. He would boil the bodies down, strap them to the side of his boat and sail back home to sell the bodies to their families for proper burial. I found him such a bizarre character that I knew he had to be in my story.

Research helps begin the framework of story.

If you look in the front of many books, you will find a list of acknowledgments where the author thanks those who helped with the book. For a mystery this might include a police department, the forensics department, the coroner, etc. etc. This is primary research and can be very useful.

However, one problem I have found though in talking to experts about their particular field is they are usually more concerned with "getting it right" than telling a story. As a novelist, telling a story is your priority. You have to listen carefully to the expert and sift through the mounds of information they are shoveling your way and pick the nuggets of gold that you can use to make your story sparkle.

My recommendation if you have to write about something you are unfamiliar with, is to "cheat". Find another fiction book that writes about the same subject and see how that author did it. I asked bestselling author Lee Child how he did his research on the military since he didn't have a military background. He said that he read Nelson DeMille and Tom Clancy a lot.

In fact, that's one of the reasons you need to read a lot and watch a lot of film is to add to your toolkit of techniques and information. Every now and then I read or see something that really strikes me as being different and I write it down and file it away my drawer of ideas. You should do the same thing when researching material for your book.

Book Dissection

Someone Has Already Done It; Let Them Help You

You've got your kernel idea; your conflict lock and you've done your research. Before you begin to write your book, you should find a novel similar to what you plan to write that is already published. I guarantee you there is something out there that is similar. Then you should sit down with your razor sharp brain and slice it apart to see all the pieces. Then put them together again to see how they all fit.

You have to ask yourself a number of questions:

1. What was the original idea the author started with? How close is it to mine?
2. How did the author translate that idea into a story? What twist did the author put on the original idea? What's my twist? How am I different from this author's work?
3. What is the theme/intent to this story? What is mine going to be?
4. Why did the author begin where he or she did? Will a similar opening work for me?
5. Why did the author choose the perspective/point of view he or she did? What will mine be?
6. What scope did he or she place on the story? What bookends? Can I have similar bookends?
7. What is the pacing of the story? How much time did it cover?
8. How did the author bring the story to a conclusion? What was the climactic scene? What is mine going to be?
9. What did the author do that you liked?
10. What did the author do that you didn't like?

11. What didn't the author put in the book that you might have? Why didn't the author put that in?
12. What was in the book that you feel could have been left out? How would the story change if it were left out?
13. What were the subplots? How did they connect with the main plot? Did all the subplots get resolved?
14. Why did the author pick the settings he or she did?

If you will notice, all the above questions relate to chapters in this book. These are questions you are going to face in your own manuscript. If you can understand how someone who successfully wrote the same type of book answered them, you greatly improve your ability to answer them.

One thing you can do is take an Excel spreadsheet. Each row in the sheet is a scene in the book you are dissecting. The first column is a brief summary of the action of that scene. The next column is the *purpose* of that scene. Do this for the entire book. Then delete the first column. Focus on the purpose column. You add a column to the right of purpose and label that my actions. You now have an outline for your book that will not plagiarize the other book.

Here's another interesting exercise to do. Take a book that was made into a film and compare the two. For example, *The Great Santini* by Pat Conroy. If you read the book, then watch the movie, you will notice several subplots are missing from the movie version that are in the book. How did the screenwriter do this yet maintain the original idea and story of the book? Did these subplots add or take away from the book?

I was talking to producer Dan Curtis (*Winds of War*) and he told me how he works on taking a novel and turning it into a screenplay. First he breaks the novel down into a list of one or two sentence summaries of every major scene or action. Then he writes the screenplay off that list. Then he breaks the screenplay down into a list of one or two sentence summaries and sees how that compares to the one he did for the novel.

Use the narrative structure in Tool 6 to lay out the structure of the novels you read. What is the hook, your initiating event? What are the progressive complications/escalating conflict? What is the choice the protagonist has to make in the moment of crisis? How is it made? How is the main plot resolved in the climactic scene? How do the subplots support the main plot?

It is essential that you be well read in the area in which you wish to write. The more you read, the more you will get imprinted in your conscious and subconscious brain the style and manner in which those types of stories are written, which will aid you greatly in writing your own.

You should also read more first novels, rather than the latest by a best-selling author. Since you are trying to get published, see what kind of novel it takes to get published. Some best-selling authors can crank out anything—which would not get published if a no-name author did it—and have it become a best seller.

Another thing that book dissection can help you with is determining how "realistic" your book needs to be and in researching your topic. For example, in most mystery novels, police procedure lies somewhere between detective shows on TV and the way it's really done. You'll find if you interview a homicide detective about how they cover a murder scene, that you'll be overwhelmed with detail and the scene you write in your book would have to be many hours long and slow your action down. So see how such scenes are generally written in most novels that are published in your genre and proceed accordingly.

I've sat down with best-sellers and breakout novels and broken them down on a spreadsheet scene by scene to study the structure. Many authors I've talked to have done something similar in order to learn.

A question you should ask yourself after dissecting a book like what you want to write is this: How is my book going to be different? What is my unique twist? Every idea has been done—it is in the development of your story off that idea that you have to bring your originality.

Outlining

Many Theories, One Concept

How do you organize your life? How do you organize your day? I submit to you that however you do that, is how you will initially approach organizing your novel. Do you outline your day? Your month? Your year? Your life? Your career?

Once you recognize this, though, remember you can always change.

I have grown fonder of outlining the more I have written. A novel is very complex when viewed in its entirety, most particularly mainstream fiction. Working without an outline is sort of "winging" it. I say this after having done that for eight straight manuscripts. I think I have finally learned my lesson and have actually gotten to the point of outlining in some degree of detail (about a page per chapter) the entire proposed novel. Or at least as far as I can project ahead. An outline is a living document that you can constantly revise and add to as need.

I'm updating the above paragraph after 45 manuscripts written and I believe even more strongly now in outlining. I think every hour spent outlining prior to starting a novel, saves you many hours in the actual writing process. It also helps you to write a better novel as you will 'tighten' down the story in your outline before you write, rather than having to do it in rewrite.

To be honest, I only outlined my first complete novel when I had a contract that called for a complete outline to be submitted to the publisher prior to final approval for the project (and more importantly a portion of the advance was to be paid on acceptance of the outline.). You are going to have to "outline" sooner or later when writing. You can do it as you go along or you can do it before you write. Doing it as you go along often causes you to have to waste a lot of time writing material that either has to be thrown out or be extensively rewritten. It is prudent to do a lot of the thinking work ahead of time.

The major problem in working without a good outline is that you tend to get "stuck" about halfway through. When I first began writing this wasn't a major problem. My stories were basic and relatively straightforward action/adventure and, while I didn't have a detailed outline, I did have a good idea of where I wanted the story to go (as they were based somewhat on personal experiences) so I managed to blunder my way through. As I tried writing more complex stories, I found myself getting stuck more and more often and having to take days away from the keyboard to work out where the story was going and keep the subplots in line.

When you start your manuscript with your one sentence original idea, you have a relatively blank slate to work with. The further along you get, the less options you have. If you work without an outline, you may find yourself with *no* options at some point. Or at least no good options. This is, to slightly understate the predicament, not good.

If you combine many of the other chapters in this book such as narrative structure, the beginning, characters, etc. you get a good overview of the pieces you need to put together a novel. Outlining is putting those pieces into a framework. The basis of your framework is that one-sentence original idea that I beat into you early in this book. Then you decide your storyline and the characters who are going to live the story.

I cannot overemphasize (OK, I probably could) how important it is to have a feel for your characters before you begin writing. I consider getting that feel part of outlining—bringing your characters to life.

Outlining is also very critical in keeping your subplots tight to the main plot. You will restrict yourself from going off in tangents if you know at which point in your main story a subplot develops and where and how it will eventually come back and tie into the main story line.

Another advantage of outlining is that since the outline is tight to start with, as you write and add flesh to your outline, you can make the story even tighter.

One of my biggest obstacles to outlining was that I just wanted to get started writing and didn't want to take a couple of weeks doing the outline. Now I realize how much time in the long run it saves me to stay away from the manuscript and do the outline first.

The degree of detail in your outline is personal. In fact, you may chose not to have one at all. But don't treat it like the gospel once you do devise one. As you go along the characters will develop a life of their own as will the story. As you fill in details, occasionally these details will cause you to change parts of your story as opposed to what was outlined. None of my recent, more complex novels, turned out the way I thought they would way back in the beginning when all I had was the original idea and some research.

Remember that outlining is an ongoing process just like the writing. If you view a novel in the beginning as a large blank slate, then the original idea is a sentence you write at the top of the page. From there you start your outline, tracing characters and events along the timeline of your story. When you feel you have an adequate outline, you start writing. As the story progresses, you must go back every once in a while and redo the outline, tightening your story down.

I view this for me as writing in surges. I project out my story as much as I know at the time. Then I proceed to write. When I sense that I am losing track, I go back over my outline and fill in what I've already written, adding in all the details. With these new details, I redo the outline, tightening down what has yet to be written and making sure it is in congruence with what has already been written. Sometimes, I also have to go back and add a layer to the story, or take a layer away.

There are some critical questions that you must answer before you begin your manuscript. Answer these questions in writing, not in your head. To me, the bottom line on outlining is writing down everything I can possibly think of with regard to the story. You will find that the process of actually writing down those great thoughts you have might knock you up against the harsh rocks of reality. Sometimes it looks very different in black and white on paper, than in color in your brain.

Here are the questions:

What is my one sentence original idea?

Who are my main characters? What are their primary motivations? Do their primary motivations naturally lead them to assume the role they must, in this novel? How did they get these primary motivations? How do I *show* the reader the characters primary motivations?

Where and when is my setting?

What point of view will tell this story best?

What tone will I have?

What should be my initiating event?

How will conflict escalate?

What will be the moment of crisis for my protagonist?

What is the climax of my story?

How do I maintain suspense/reader interest throughout the novel?

Caveat. Be careful that your writing doesn't appear to be just a blown up outline. When that happens, the writing appears to be stilted and a little forced. Also, just expanding an outline leaves little room for creativity and allowing the characters to react and "live". You may have outlined certain events occurring, but when you actually sit down and write your characters experiencing those events, usually you will find that it turns out not exactly as outlined. Sort of like real life. Go with it. Allow your characters to be living beings involved in the story.

Find the degree of outlining that you are comfortable with, but at least consider doing some sort of outline. There are some very successful authors who can break a novel down by sections and structure and crank out certain genre novels according to a "script" they have for that type of book. And, although many don't like hearing it, there is a formula to some type of novels. Although we all want to be original (or maybe we don't?), realize that if you are writing a romance and you produce something totally unlike any other romance on the bookshelves you've done two things: you haven't written a romance in the first place, and secondly, when you try to market it, it won't be viewed as a romance. You may be the trailblazer like those I mentioned earlier and start a new field, but the odds aren't good. If you feel strongly about your writing, don't let that dissuade you, just be aware of the reality of the situation.

I definitely feel that updating your outline is important every day when you sit down and try to write chapters. Pick a start point and an end point for every chapter. Then ask yourself how do I get from one to the other? What is the purpose of this chapter? Also look at the chapter in terms of the overall story. Where does it fit? Is this the right time for this to happen? If you don't have a definite end point, your chapter will meander.

Appendix 1 is an example of a chapter outline for *Area 51*. While some of the notes might not make sense to you, they certainly do to me because I did the research and know what the original idea is. The keys things to note are:

I list the date at the top, putting it in time sequence for the story.

I have the characters who will be in the chapter (which makes me cross-reference to my character summaries.)

I list the events in sequence, giving the major action and where it occurs.

I make notes on key material that must be dealt with later, in other chapters, or already has been dealt with. This is very important to insure continuity of story.

I have a definite start point at the beginning of the event sequence and a definite end-point. I have listed all important events that I need to occur in between.

Perhaps most importantly I give the *purpose* of the chapter. Where does it fit in the overall story? How does it relate to the original idea? This will prevent having extraneous material.

This isn't to say that once I start writing the chapter things won't change. But it's a heck of a lot easier to write with all the information thought out beforehand rather than making it up as I go. Basically what I'm saying is that the outline allows you to concentrate on the writing since you know what you are going to put down. I find my writing is better when I have a good outline.

An outline will grow out of your original idea when you start doing your research. For me, research is one of the "fun" parts of my job. Going to the library and looking through the stacks, checking magazines, videos, the computer, etc. all are interesting. Keep your eyes open. Just because you are looking for a book filed under U410.L1 E38, doesn't mean you ignore the books to the left and right of it. I usually scan all the books that are shelved together and have often come up with goldmines of information sitting three books over from what I thought I needed.

A last word on the Catch-22 of outlining. Not to contradict what I've written above, but there is a problem with trying to sit down and outline your very first manuscript. The problem is that since *you've never written a manuscript, you are trying to outline something you've never done.*

I opened this section by saying that I have grown more fond of outlining the more I have written, but that's also a natural outgrowth of gaining more experience in novel structure and style. I've learned enough in writing manuscripts that I am able to outline much better now. I don't think I would have done anywhere as good a job on outlining my first manuscript. This is also why I emphasize starting out writing about something you know quite a bit about and keeping the story as simple as possible.

My recommendation on outlining is simple: *write down everything you think you know about your book*. I say "think you know" because the transition from what you think are startlingly clear thoughts to black and white on paper can be very difficult. I've had great ideas that I believed would make great stories, but when I start actually sketching it out in the real world—on paper or on computer—rather than in my head, I find things change considerably.

One phrase I always say is: *Details drive the story*. This is why, even with an outline, a story takes on a life of its own. No matter how detailed you outline, you can't think of everything. As you actually write the story, details will start popping up that will cause you to make changes. Most of the time these are details of reality or fact that can't be changed.

For example, in your thriller you have a scene where your protagonist is searching a series of tunnels, looking for the bad guys. The way you wrote your outline, the bad guy isn't in the tunnel and your secondary main character is sitting in her car on the surface and she sees the bad guy escape. So she calls the protagonist on the radio and he rushes to the surface for your climactic scene hanging off the skid of the helicopter, right? Wrong. You can't use radio to get hold of someone underground. Or cell phones. This is a detail you might not have thought of when doing your outline but as you write it you realize it. So you change, you adjust.

Just as details can limit you, they can also give you more opportunities. This goes back to research being an ongoing process.

If you've been following the flow of this book, they represent the way you might want to consider approaching your manuscript. You've done a lot of legwork that you can put together to begin your outline at this point.

Do you have to outline?
Genre can make a difference:

Thrillers/Suspense/Mysteries usually rely more heavily on plot.
Science Fiction/Fantasy usually needs world-building.
Literary/Romance rely more heavily on character so plot might have to follow out of character.

When outlining, you are usually listing scenes. It's important to know exactly what a scene is. A scene is a unit of action with its own start point and end point and has all five elements of narrative structure in it that we will cover under plot. A scene has its own protagonist and antagonist, not necessarily the same as the books. A scene should be one time, one place. If you jump time or place, you usually end up with a new scene. Time jumps inside a scene are difficult to handle because the reader will wonder what happened in the time that was just fast-forwarded over. Also, you can confuse the reader, and that's something we never want to do. Characters and story should come out of a scene changed. There must be conflict in every scene, as noted earlier.

We're storytellers, the oldest profession, not newspaper reporters. We're not just relating facts. We're entertaining and involving the reader in the story. So write scenes, not incidents.

One lesson I learned from screenwriting was a good rule of thumb: Start as far in the action as possible. Both in the story and in scenes. In *Chasing the Ghost*, I originally opened the book, and the first scene, with Horace Chase sitting in a cop bar in Boulder, Colorado. On the TV they're reporting that a state trooper has been killed. Chase's red beeper goes off. Everyone knows he's on the Federal counter-terrorist task force. Chase drives home, grabs his rucksack and sniper rifle, drives to the airfield and gets picked up by helicopter. En route to Montana where they know the killers are heading he's briefed by his team leader and given authorization to shoot to kill on sight. He's dropped off on a snow-covered ridgeline and sets up his sniper rifle. It took me sixteen pages to get him there and I have five setting shifts—bar to home to helipad to helicopter to ridgeline.

I cut those sixteen pages and open the book to the scene with him sitting on that ridgeline looking through his sniper rifle. Much more exciting and a tight scene.

The number one thing you must know about every scene is: What is the purpose of this scene? How does it support my kernel idea?

The Following Are Tools That Might Help You In Your Day-To-Day Writing And Will Help You Develop Your Process As A Novelist:

A Master Character List

A master list with descriptions and history of each person in your book. Every time you use a name, write it down and give a brief description, even if you think it is a character you will never use again in the manuscript. I don't know how many times I've had to go searching back, looking for the name of that minor character that I used somewhere in the first hundred pages and who suddenly, unexpectedly, reappears in chapter 23. It helps considerably to have this character work done *prior* to starting the novel—more on this in Tool Five Characters.

I've also used the same name for different characters in the course of a manuscript, which is another good reason to keep track.

In a similar way, write down any 'fact' you make up or use so you can keep track of it.

Maps Of Locales

If you can't stay oriented, your reader can't either. When I read *Lonesome Dove*, I had my atlas and followed the herd from the Mexico-Texas border all the way up north to Montana. As an author, you have to do the same thing. I own—let's see as I look about—at least eight different maps/atlases within handy reach, including:

The Rand McNally Universal World Atlas
The Times Atlas of World History
The Universal World Atlas
Rand McNally Road Atlas of the US
Rand McNally Road Atlas of Europe
The Atlas of Earth Mysteries
The Atlas of the Second World War

The West Point Atlas of American Wars

A Michelin map of "Africa: Central and South; Madagascar." (This is specific for a certain book I'm currently working on)

A geographic map of a section of the Rocky Mountains (again for a specific project)

I just bought a $200 atlas at my local bookstore because I have found maps to be critical to my stories. I always end up having to look up very strange and rare places. Know where Ngorongoro Crater is? I used it in an *Area 51* book and I didn't know where it was either until I tracked it down in an atlas. You can also use Google maps online.

Not only do these atlases and maps give me locales, they give histories and facts about the locales that often become essential to the story. When I get detail oriented in action scenes I use topographic maps to give me a feel for terrain. Maps are also useful in determining distances—remember people do take time to travel—unless of course you're writing science fiction in which case—well, make sure your rules work and remain consistent within the covers of the book when your spaceship hits warp drive.

There are certain genres where maps are very important. If you've ever read *The Lord of the Rings* you know where the Shire is in relation to Mordor and the land in between that Frodo has to traverse. If you write historical fiction people want to know what the political boundaries of the time were and where those major battles took place. Do you know where Shiloh is? What river it's next to?

Also, and I shudder to mention this, there are people who don't exactly know where, let's say, Madagascar, is.

When I was in Special Forces, before we went to another country, we did what we called an "area study". We spent time learning everything we could about the place: topography, weather, customs, languages, religions, etc. etc. As a writer I do the same thing when I write about a place.

Diagrams Of Important Places—I.E. Houses, The Rooms, Etc.

Again, to keep you oriented. If you can't stay oriented, your reader certainly won't be able to. If your main character turns left into the bedroom for the first 15 chapters and you make a mistake and have her turning right in chapter 16, there is no doubt but that it will be noticed. One thing about a book—the reader can always turn back and check your information.

Story Grid (Appendix 2)

This keeps you oriented and allows you to go back and find certain passages quicker than having to reread the entire manuscript. For the type of stories I write, it's extremely important to be able to keep track of location, time, characters and action.

Take a look at the Appendix. From left to right across the top I have the chapter, the starting page number, the ending page number, the date and day of the week (which can be quite important.), the location of the action, the local time, the Zulu time, and a brief description of what happens.

Zulu time is Greenwich Mean Time. Remember that while it's noon in Washington it is nighttime in Tokyo and you can't fly between the two in 30 minutes (unless you're writing science fiction, of course).

Different time zones can become critical to some types of stories. Quick quiz: What is the only place on Earth that has no time zone?

Answer: Antarctica
Quiz: What place on Earth is on a half hour time zone?
Answer: Central Australia

When I deployed overseas in Special Forces we wore two watches, one on each wrist. One had the local time wherever we were and the other was set to Zulu time. The latter was the time we used to coordinate all messages, resupplies, operations, etc. with higher headquarters, which was usually in a different time zone than we were.

I know this story grid doesn't seem like the most artistic thing in the world, but I find it very important for me because it keeps me oriented to the details of the story as I write. While writing is a creative task, I find writing a novel also requires quite a bit of organizational ability and sometimes it's difficult to find the two traits in the same person. Once you start your story—and I will go into this in more detail later on—the story takes on a life of its own and in a paradoxical manner, your creativity is limited by your creation growing on its own.

The story grid is not an outline. It is filled in as the manuscript is written to allow me to keep track of what I've already done. I find it to be particularly helpful when rewriting. As you will see when we get to subplots, when you change one aspect of a novel, it tends to change things in other places. It's easier to realize and find these other places using the story grid.

Summaries Of Important Information

I summarize research articles and books, writing the important information (along with source and page numbers) down in bullets on one page that I can quickly scan. Sometimes when my story stalls out, I look through the "bullet" pages of information and am reminded of some piece of information that allows me to rejuvenate the story line. Remember that class on research that you had in school so many years ago? The same applies to writing fiction.

I keep saying the details drive a story, and the more information you have, the more details you have. Large sections of some of my books are based on facts that readers think are fiction.

Newspaper/Magazine Articles/Online Articles/Blogs

I can take any newspaper and come up with two or three book ideas from the front page (just like in the scene in *The Player*). Articles can give you great background information.

What I particularly like about articles is that they do a lot of the research for you, summarizing information. I index excerpts and place them in three ring binders for handy reference. You can use Scrivener or some other program to index hyperlinks to key information. It might be very fresh in your mind today when you read that article but five months from now when you're in the middle of writing chapter 27 you'll be lucky if you can even remember reading the article, never mind what was in it—writing a novel is a *long* process.

Videotapes/DVDs/YouTube

When I was writing about Ayers Rock in Australia (*The Rock*) I was writing about a place I'd never been to. I did not have the funds or the time to fly to Australia to research an idea that I had not sold, so I did the next best thing. I rented travel videos and toured the country via my TV. I was able to sit at my desk and describe scenes as I watched them.

Of course I didn't have the actual feel of the place, but I could gain some of that by researching travel accounts of people who *had* been there. Ask around—you'd be amazed at the people in your neighborhood who've gone to the strangest places or have had the weirdest experiences.

In the same manner, I just watched a video on the search for Atlantis and was able to see some of the potential locales for another one of my manuscripts. You can learn about firearms, medical procedures, bungee jumping, hang gliding, etc. etc. all from videos. Naturally it is best to actually go to the locales and do the action yourself so you can write about it validly, but when that isn't possible, this can be the next best thing.

The Discovery Channel constantly amazes me. I DVR when something interesting comes on. It's kind of neat to be writing a book that has the Great Pyramid in it, and while writing, a two hour special on the Great Pyramid comes on TV. In the same manner, if you want to know about life on board an aircraft carrier, paddling up the Amazon, etc., sooner or later, it comes on TV.

In fact, videos can give you information that you can't get any other way. I wrote a manuscript that had the Golden Gate Bridge figuring prominently in the story. I bought a video on the making of the bridge and was able to see things that there was no other way to see.

There are videos on just about everything and everyplace on YouTube. I filmed a bunch of short clips while visiting Shiloh and have been posting them on YouTube, so that someone researching Shiloh can actually see places there, such as the Hornet's Nest.

Bookmarked web pages and printed copies of important facts form various sources are useful.

Indexed Binders

Filled with most of the above information in it so you can find it when needed. Having stacks of information that aren't organized does you little good.

Use whatever format works for you. WRITE IT DOWN.

Tool 4: Point of View and Voice

After many years of writing and teaching novel writing, I firmly believe that perspective or point of view is the number one style problem for most writers. It is also one of the easiest problems to correct with awareness of both the problem and possible solutions. For the sake of simplicity, in this chapter I will stick with the term point of view, although it is interchangeable with perspective.

Here's a question: What is reality? Ultimately it's what someone perceives it to be. Thus there is no one, singular reality among people. Thus your choice of the point with which to tell your story taints the story for the reader. The same story told from two different points of view is a very different story.

In real life if three people see an event, you have three different points of view. When writing your novel, the point of view the author chooses to channel the scene through is the point of view the reader gets.

So who is telling the story? You are. But whose voice does the reader 'hear' when they read? The point of view through which you relate the story. It could be yours in omniscient voice, or channeled through various characters in third limited, or simply be a narrator telling a story in first person.

When considering how to tell your story, the first thing you have to do is select a point of view. This may be the most critical decision you have to make. Often the type of story you are writing will clearly dictate the point of view, but a good understanding of the various modes of presentation is essential because this is one area where beginning novelists often have problems. They may select the right point of view, but it is often used poorly because of a lack of understanding of the tool itself.

Regardless of which point of view (or points of view) you choose to use, there is one thing you must have: *you* as the author must have a good feeling about the point of view with which you are telling the story. If you don't have a warm and fuzzy about that, this confusion will most definitely be translated to the reader. Remember, ultimately, point of view is your voice as a writer.

Some people write like a music video: point of view flying all over the place, giving glimpses into each character but never really keeping the reader oriented. I say this because the best analogy I can give for point of view is to look at it as your camera. You as author are the director: you see and know everything in your story. But the reader only sees and knows what the camera records: the point of view you choose. You must always keep that in mind. You see the entire scene, but your lens only records the words you put on the page and you have to keep your lens tightly focused and firmly in hand.

The key term to know, like a director, is the word 'cut'. A cut in film terminology is when the camera is either a) stopped, then restarted later, or b) stopped and another camera is then used. To a writer, a cut is a change in point of view. In a music video, they go about three seconds before having to 'cut'. Robert Altman, in the beginning of *The Player*, uses an extremely long single camera sequence before the first cut—another reason to watch the film.

The most critical thing to remember about point of view is that you have to keep the reader oriented. The reader has got to know from what point of view they are viewing the scene. Lose that and you lose the reader. Thus, as with everything else, there is no wrong point of view to write in, or even mixture of point of views to write in, but it is wrong to confuse the reader as to the point of view through which they are 'seeing' the story.

Take the camera point of view a bit further. When directors do a scene, they immediately look into a viewfinder and watch the recording of the take. They do this because, although they saw what happened, they have to know what the camera recorded. As an author, you have to get out of your own point of view as the writer and be able to see what you write as the reader sees it.

1st, 3rd Limited and Omniscient Voice

First person means you use the word "I" quite a bit. It's giving the camera to one character and letting that character film a documentary while doing a voiceover.

This point of view has its advantage in that the narrator is telling his/her own story. The major disadvantage is that the reader can only see and know what the narrator experiences and knows. You, as the author, are absent in this mode, thus you surrender part of your control in writing. Remember, the first person narrator is not you the author, but rather the character in the story. The narrator can be a witness or a participant in the story.

Note that there are certain types of genre that fit first person very well, most particularly mysteries/detective stories. That's logical if you understand the advantages of first person: by using that mode, the writer can bring the reader along for the ride, disclosing clues as the narrator discovers them.

The major disadvantage of first person is that your narrator has to be present in every scene. Because of this, many writers make their narrator the protagonist. A problem can crop up in that the narrator will then be a critical part of the plot and have many things happen to them and around them. Will the narrator be able to react realistically while still telling the story in a coherent form?

Another problem can be the logistics of getting your narrator to all the key events in order to narrate them. I have seen writers end up with very convoluted, and unrealistic plots in order to do that. If the narrator isn't present at these important scenes, then they find out about them by other means, which can lessen suspense and definitely lessens the immediacy of the action in the story as you have major action occurring offstage.

Some authors use a narrator who isn't one of the main characters—what is known as a detached narrator. The narrator is more of an observer. This has some advantages. Think of the *Sherlock Holmes* stories—who is narrating? Watson. Why? Because this allows the author to withhold what Holmes is thinking from the audience.

Something else to think about—should the reader believe your narrator? If everything your narrator says is fact, then there might not be much suspense. But think about the movie *The Usual Suspects*. The story is narrated by a character, who it turns out, is the man everyone is searching for. In a book, you can raise suspense if your first person narrator is caught in a small lie early on in the story—the reader will then have to be more judgmental about everything else the narrator says.

Another big issue of first person narration is the issue of tense and time. There are two ways to view time in a first person story:

I remember when. In this case, the narrator is telling the story in past tense, looking backward. This immediately reduces the suspense of whether the narrator survives the story. There is also the issue that the narrator is thus withholding information from the reader—the narrator obviously knows the ending, yet chooses not to reveal it to the reader.

In real time. The narrator is telling the story as it unfolds around him or her. A problem with this is what happens when the narrator is involved in an emotionally overwhelming event? Will he still be able to narrate the story?

The big problem with time sense is that even the best writers tend to mix 1 and 2 above. At times they will be in real time, then every so often slip into past time. Additionally, to give you an even bigger headache, both are usually written in past tense. So how do you write a real time story in past tense?

A further problem with first person is many writers tend to slide from first into second person point of view. Any time you put *you* in your narrative, addressing the reader, you have moved from first to second person.

There are ways to get around the disadvantages of first person. Examine some first person novels and you will discover them. *Interview With A Vampire* by Anne Rice is an interesting use of first person and the title tells you why. She has the first person of the reporter start the story but shifts into a first person narrative by the vampire Louis through the medium of the interview. She can go back in time with Louis and then return to the present with the reporter, both in first person. She has two levels of interest and suspense: the present fate of the narrator, and the fate of the vampire in his own tale.

There are other novelists who have come up with novel ideas (pun intended) to tell first person stories while getting around some of the disadvantages. Present tense is an option.

I place great emphasis in my own writing career and when teaching upon reading and also upon watching movies/videos, but I watch videos and read books in a different mode as a "writer." I study them for structure. To see what the author/ screenwriter/ director did with the subject matter. How it was presented. When you pick up a novel, the first thing you should note is what person it is written in. Then ask yourself why the author chooses that point of view. What did the novel gain from that point of view?

When I give examples in a little bit, you will see more clearly the advantages and disadvantages of first person.

One thing about first person to keep in mind. It is the voice most novice writers naturally gravitate to, but it is one of the most difficult voices to do well. Because of that, there is an initial negative impression among agents and editors when confronted with a first person story.

First Person
Most limiting
Narrator is not the author
The narrator always has the camera
Narrator has to be present in every scene or get information second-hand
Works for mysteries
Hard for thrillers
Detached narrator: *Sherlock Holmes*
Believable narrator: *The Usual Suspects*

First Person Time Sense
I remember when . . .
Already know what happened and are withholding
No suspense over fate of the narrator
In real time
Come along with me
Emotionally overwhelming events
Both are usually told in past tense. which further confuses things
You usually end up mixing the two modes

Third Person Limited
Is when you give the camera to various characters and they record the scene. Everything in the book is channeled through your point of view characters.

A key concept here is the concept of a 'cut'. When a film director yells cut, he means one of several things: first, in all cases, he's stopping the camera that is currently filming. Then he is going to:

Leave the camera with the current point of view character, but is moving that character off-screen to another time and/or place and then restarting the camera.

Take the camera from the current point of view character and give it to another character who will then 'film' the scene. This scene could be in the same place or a different place. It could be the same time or a different time. If it's the same time, then the reader is getting the same scene from different POV characters and you must have a very good reason for doing that because it's head-hopping.

Regardless, what you *must* do is make sure the reader knows you, as the author, have done a cut. The reader must know within the first paragraph after a cut which character now has the camera. I recommend against doing a cut in the middle of a scene unless you have a specific purpose for doing so.

Another factor in third limited is that each point of view character is literally going to have a different point of view. Each is going to see the same situation differently. As the author this requires you to shift your perspective as you write to the various POV characters and even write each one slightly different in terms of style.

There are what I call first-third stories, where the book is written in third limited, but there is only one point of view character. An author might choose to do this as an alternative to the problems of first person POV.

How many points of view can you handle? Exactly how schizophrenic are you? It's a question of your ability as a writer. If you aren't an expert at POV I'd recommend limiting the number of POV characters as much as possible. One thing I stayed away from in my thrillers was getting into the POV of the antagonist. Because the antagonist knows his dastardly plan and I don't want to reveal it to the reader. Remember, you can't cheat your reader by going into the POV of a character and withhold information they know from the reader.

There are several problems with too many POV characters beyond just your ability. If you have too many POVs, you will reveal a lot of information to the reader, but not to the other characters. Thus your reader will end up knowing more than your characters, which could end up being an awkward situation as you try to get some characters up to speed on information they need to know but which the reader already knows. You could end up writing some really boring scenes for the reader.

Another problem with too many POV characters is you diffuse attention from your protagonist. The reader spends so much time in points of view outside of the main character that they lose focus.

Third Person Limited
Everything is channeled through various characters' points of view
Cuts have to be very clear to readers
Each POV character must be distinct
First, third stories
Cutting in the middle of a scene: is there a purpose
How many points of view can you—and the reader—handle
Too many POV characters: The reader ends up knowing more than any of the characters
Diffuse attention from your protagonist
The line between Third Limited and Omniscient is a thin one

Omniscient point of view. This is also known as authorial narrative. When I first began writing I felt I had to lock in third person on a character for every scene. And that worked. But the more I wrote, the more I wanted to use an omniscient point of view. I also realized that most of my favorite authors wrote in omniscient voice.

I liken authorial point of view to the camera getting pulled back in the hands of the author in order to show the viewer more. There are times you might want to pull back so you can tell the reader more information or show the reader more than the characters who are in the scene might be able to see or know.

For example, a battle scene can be written much better from omniscient point of view if you want the reader to understand the battle. But if you want the reader to see how one specific character is responding to the danger of combat, you might stick with third person from that character's point of view.

One of the most difficult obstacles for me as a writer was accepting that I could write from the authorial point of view. That I can describe things as they are or were using my own voice as the author of the work. The more I write, the more I find it important to be able to do this. There may be some information that is not going to fit using third person. Also, you may get very tired of writing "he thought" over and over again and the reader may grow weary of seeing it.

Starting sentences with the word THE shifts you up into omniscient quite a bit.

Omniscient
Authorial narrative
Camera is above, all-seeing and all-knowing
Must be the story psychologist
Good for action scenes
Be careful of head-hopping
More authoritative

You have to consider point of view before you begin your book and before you write every scene, much as a movie director has to. You have to determine the best point of view to get across to the reader the story you are trying to tell. Decide where are you going to place the camera to the best advantage of the story.

Say you are going to write a thriller about a female FBI agent tracking down a vicious serial killer. You want to open your book with a scene that will grab the reader and set the stage for the suspense of the novel so you decide to open with a killing. What point of view will you use? Now, remember, no point of view is *wrong*—you just have to understand the advantages and disadvantages of your possible choices and make a knowledgeable decision. And remember, you will most likely be stuck with that point of view for the entire manuscript.

First person might be a bit difficult. After all, this would most likely mean your narrator actually witnesses the scene. This isn't impossible, but it could be awkward. Perhaps you use first person from the protagonist's point of view and she witnesses the murder but is not in a position to take any action? Using first person from the POV of the victim means the book is rather short, unless the victim survives the attack and swears vengeance. First person from the killer would make for a dark book, but it has been done.

You can decide to use third person from the point of view of the victim. This can build tension well, but also means the chapter will end abruptly.

You can use third person from the point of view of the killer, but remember that the killer knows who he or she is and therefore you have to be careful how much insight into the killer's head you allow. A technique some use to overcome that limitation is to have the killer think of himself in different terms than his reality. The killer is Joe Schmo, but when he's in killer mode he thinks of himself as Captain Hook, thus hiding his identity from the reader in third person insight.

Or, you could use omniscient, placing your 'camera' above the scene. Here, though, you have to be careful not to show too much and give away the killer's identity. Much like a director might choose a dark basement where the viewer can't see the killer's face, you will do the same.

Another example of considering how to write a scene is if you have two characters meeting in a pub for an important exchange of dialogue. They sit across from each other. How are you going to 'shoot' this scene? From third person of one of the characters? That means you get that character's thoughts and you describe the other character's reactions—i.e. the camera is on your POV character's shoulder. Is it important that the reader know one character's thought more than the other's? Or is it more important to show one character's reactions than the others?

Or, do you keep switching the camera back and forth across the booth, going from one to the other? If you're Larry McMurty and won a Pulitzer Prize you might be able to do that, but for most of us, such a constant switching of POV is very disconcerting to the reader. Or do you shoot it omniscient with the camera off to the side and simply show actions and record dialogue?

Consider this scene like a date. If you were out with someone and you knew exactly what they were thinking, and they knew what you were thinking, would there be any suspense to the date? Taking too many points of view can greatly reduce your suspense.

I've written in all the above points of view. I tend to go with omniscient now as it's the voice that works best for me, but it took me almost forty manuscripts to figure that out.

Examples

First: Years ago, I was told that to be an effective sniper, I had to be a man who could shoot another human being on nothing but an order and stop; also on order. The stopping is important. I'd been told I was one of those people.

Third: Years ago, Horace Chase was told that an effective sniper was a man who could shoot another human being on nothing but an order and stop; also on order. The stopping is important. He knew he was one of those people.

Omniscient: An effective sniper is a man who can shoot another human being on nothing but an order and stop; also on order. The stopping is important. Horace Chase was one of those people and that made him dangerous.

Note the subtle differences in each POV for this opening line from *Chasing The Ghost*. In the first one we're getting it all through Chase. In the second one, it's through Chase, but with more distance. In the last, it's omniscient and the last line part is more definitive with the author telling you he *is* one of those people. Not that he'd been told or that he knew he was.

A Deeper Look at POV

Here is the difference between an expository scene in third person limited and omniscient:

Third Person

Joe walked up the dirt road leading to the Giza Plateau. As he cleared the rise he saw the Sphinx off to his right and the three massive pyramids ahead. He knew that historians believed the largest of the three had been built by the Pharaoh Khufu, more popularly known as Cheops. He'd read that it was 138 meters high. He was impressed with the magnitude of the construction, noting the massive blocks of aged stone and wondering how they had been moved so long ago.

Omniscient

Joe walked up the dirt road leading to the Giza Plateau. The Sphinx was to his right and the three massive pyramids in front. Historians believe the largest pyramid was built by the Pharaoh Khufu, more popularly known as Cheops. It is 138 meters high, built of massive blocks of aged stone that must have taken a marvel of engineering to move.

The second presents the information directly, without having to be processed through Joe's head. If you want to break yourself of always using a character's point of view to write, try using the word THE to start sentences. This will help you in writing narrative. Remember that you are the AUTHOR. You can actually write down what you want to say without having to have it come from the point of view of one of your characters.

For more examples of the various points of views try to visualize the following: Your point of view character, Joe, is sitting in a room looking out a window into a courtyard. Two men walk into the courtyard, speaking to each other. They proceed to get into a fight. Notice the various ways I can write this scene:

First Person

I saw the two people walk into the courtyard. They began to argue with each other, and then suddenly, they began to fight.

Note: Because I wasn't out there, I couldn't hear what they said, which is a limitation of first person. However, I could find out what was said later on by talking to one of the two people. (There are always ways to get around disadvantages.) Or, I could change the story and have my first person character in the courtyard in order to be able to relate what happens—but the presence of that character in the courtyard could also change what occurs.

Another issue is identifying the two men. My narrator would have to know them in order to do that.

If I changed the story and made my narrator either of the characters, then the issue would be whether I am telling this as it occurs, or looking back. If I am telling as it occurs, then can my narrator still narrate what is happening coherently while in the middle of participating in a fight?

Third Person, Locked Point Of View

It is as if you are telling the reader what is happening out there from Joe's point of view and he knows something about what is happening:

Joe saw John walk into the courtyard with Ted. Joe could see that they were arguing and he knew they were still probably upset about their earlier confrontation over Madeline's boyfriend.

He saw John hold up his hands in a placating manner and say something. Then he noticed that Ted was yelling something back and John dropped his hands.

Joe jumped to his feet as he saw John grab the collar of Ted's windbreaker.

Note that everything that happens is being filtered through Joe's senses. And we have to 'trust' Joe's assumptions about the scene; for example, that the two are upset over the earlier confrontation. For all Joe knows, it might be something very different.

What many writers do to overcome this is use one of the advantages of third person, which is switch POVs from one character to another who has a better camera angle.

Third Person, Shifting Point Of View

The same scene. We start in Joe's point of view, and then shift when it is necessary.

Joe looked up from his cup of coffee and saw John and Ted walk into the courtyard. Joe could see that they were arguing. He assumed the two were still upset about their earlier confrontation over Madeline's boyfriend.

In the courtyard, John could see Joe watching them but he could care less. John was still uneasy about their earlier confrontation over Madeline's boyfriend.

"I still don't accept it," Ted muttered. "It's wrong."

John held up his hands. "I don't want to talk about it any more. We've discussed Philip enough. It's up to Madeline."

"No, it's not up to Madeline. We have a responsibility. He's not good for her and I don't approve of their going out together."

John dropped his hands and glared at Ted; he could never just let anything go. "I said, I don't want to talk about it again. Period."

Ted wasn't to be dissuaded. "We have to. I think--"

John felt something snap inside of him and he grabbed the collar of Ted's windbreaker. "Goddamn it. I told you I didn't want to talk about it again."

Note: here I describe what is happening in the courtyard by getting into one of the two men's heads. Note that I make sure the reader knows I've shifted character POV by reversing the camera angle. I let the reader know a little background simply by having one of the character's thinking about it. We can hear what is said and we know what the argument is about. The camera is on John's shoulder with a feed into his brain. We know who the characters are because John, the POV character, knows. We also know that what Joe suspected was true, by having John confirm what they were fighting about. But there is a head hop in this scene which is a bit disconcerting, isn't it?

How do you let a reader know the POV has shifted in third person? The subject of the sentence identifies the POV.

Omniscient (author as narrator), here the author simply records observations, showing, not telling:

John and Ted walked into the courtyard. Ted's face was tight, his forehead wrinkled in thought, his eyes smoldering. "I still don't accept it. It's wrong."

John held up his hands. "I don't want to talk about it any more. We've discussed Philip enough. It's up to Madeline."

"No, it's not up to Madeline. We have a responsibility. He's not good for her and I don't approve of their going out together."

John dropped his hands and glared at Ted. "I said, I don't want to talk about it again. Period."

Ted wasn't to be dissuaded. "We have to. I think--"

John's hands shot up and his fingers wrapped around the collar of Ted's windbreaker. "Goddamn it. I told you I didn't want to talk about it again."

I manage to impart all the information needed and describe the scene. The best way to describe this point of view is to pretend you, as author, are a movie camera that can move around freely throughout your scenes, you show. Also, and this is difficult for new writers, you can make authorial comments such as Ted not being dissuaded because, as God, you know what everyone is thinking.

You could also write this scene with an omniscient point of view and give *both* characters' thoughts and inner reactions.

Note that in first person, because I had the glass between the character, and me I couldn't hear what they said. If I was in the court-yard with them, so I could hear what was being said, I also might affect the action, because of my presence. In third person I am free to either lock onto one of the characters. In omniscient I am floating overhead, and not affecting the scene at all.

The bottom line is: Every time you use a point of view, make sure you look at the advantages and disadvantages. Recognize what information you are imparting and ultimately try to see things from the reader's point of view. In the final analysis, you must make sure your reader is smoothly imparted the information you wish for him or her to have.

More On Point Of View

Staying in a character's head also makes your character incon-sistent if the thoughts are not in line with what he/she says or does. And if it is in line, then why have to tell thoughts when the words/actions will speak for them? That isn't to say don't get into thoughts at all, but don't do it exclusively.

When you do have your characters' thoughts, make sure they think differently from each other. Don't write the same way for every one and have them react the same or they appear to be cardboard cutouts.

A word on **2d person**. It has been used but is difficult to work with. 2d person is using "you" or "we" in telling the story. This has an advantage in that it can bring the reader into the story more intimately, in fact, making the reader part of the story in the role of participant or close observer. There are occasions where the author might address the reader using 2d person.

TEST: What point of view is this book in?

ANSWER: 2d person.

Why did I choose that point of view? Because I wanted you to be involved when you read it. I wanted you the reader to feel that I was talking directly to you.

How about *mixing* the various points of views in the same novel? Can it be done?

Remember my premise: there is no wrong way. Yes, it can be done. A certain fellow named William Faulkner did an OK job of it in a novel called *The Sound And The Fury*. The first three sections of that book were first person (indeed, three different first persons). The last third person. You can do anything that works. It certainly worked for Faulkner, but remember: SMOOTHNESS.

I just finished rereading *The Last Picture Show* by Larry McMurty and in the forward he presented an interesting angle on point of view. He said that on occasion he has written a story in first person and then rewritten it in third. I've tried it and it's not as hard as you would think. What's curious though, is that in going from first, the initial rewrite turned out to be omniscient. Then I had to write down from omniscient to third. This indicates that first and omniscient can lend themselves to info-dump, which is not a good thing and something you have to be careful of. In strict third limited, you can never have even a sentence of info-dump.

When you watch TV or film, start paying very close attention how the director filmed the scene. Think about something as simple as two people sitting in a booth at a restaurant. Does the director film it from the side, showing both people? Or does the camera shift back and forth from one side of the table to the other? And if it does, when do the shifts take place? Does the director want to show the person speaking or the person listening and reacting to the other's words?

Do you see how many different ways a scene can be filmed? You, as the author, can write the same scene many different ways.

Please don't think from all that I have written above that it's wrong to get in your characters' heads. If you go into the bookstore today and pull the top ten fiction novels off the shelf, I think more than half would have varying degrees of insight into the characters' thoughts and feelings. The key is to do it right. I have emphasized this point because I have found this area to be the number one style problem for new writers. I think as long as you are aware of it and use the tool properly, you will be all right.

Remember: consistency and smoothness.

The most important thing about any point of view you use is that the reader knows where the 'camera' is.

What point of view do you think you've written your manuscript in?

Point Of View And Character Arc

Pull all your same character POV scenes and look at them separate from the other POV character scenes

Check to make sure the voice is consistent

Check for character arc

Point Of View and Voice

The filter over the camera lens

All voices must be distinctive

In third, the voice must change slightly for each POV character

In omniscient the voice must be knowledgeable

Every writer must find their own voice

■ ■ ■

Tool 5: People
The World: Character

The Supremacy of Character

Characters are the emotional punch of the novel.

You've probably heard it said that there are two ways to write a book. The first is to come up with a plot and then find characters to live the story. The second is to come up with characters and write their story. I squirm out of that by saying do both. Remember one thing though—it will be people who read your book and people identify primarily with people, not plots or facts. Another thing to consider is this: many times, your characters *are* your plot.

Regardless, you need people in your story. Or maybe aliens. Or an interesting rabbit such as in *Watership Down*. Or perhaps a wisteria vine as in Clyde Edgerton's *Floatplane Notebooks*. You need characters, even if they are inanimate. The antagonists in Krakauer's book *Into Thin Air* are the weather and Mount Everest, although ultimately, it is the people themselves—who chooses to climb a mountain where you know one out of six will die?

I remember in the army we used to get asked which came first: the mission or the men? The approved solution was the mission (read plot). My answer was always the men (read characters), because without the men you couldn't accomplish the mission. In the same manner, you need good characters regardless of the story, and if you keep them "in character" they will dictate what is going to happen in your story because they will react appropriately and not according to your whims as the author.

One of my other non-fiction books, *Who Dares Wins: The Green Beret Way To Conquer Fear And Succeed*, focuses on the fact that what makes the Special Forces elite is the emphasis on the men, not the mission, because without the men, the mission could not even be attempted. I think the same is true of writing— what makes a story rise above the ordinary is the emphasis on the people inhabiting it.

I was slow to appreciate the importance—indeed the pre-eminence—of characters in a novel. It was a three-stage process. First, I had to accept that characters were the most important aspect of the story. For many that's a given, but coming from a background where plot ruled, this meant I had to make a 180 degree turn in perspective. I've found the opposite is true also. I've read manuscripts that were so character oriented there was little to no plot. There are writers who need to understand the importance of having a story in which the characters exist.

The second step was to spend as much time developing my characters *before* starting the novel as I spent outlining my plot. Some people might be able to invent plot or characters on the fly as they write, but I find the time spent before starting, is time well invested. The key characters have to be alive and real to me before I write the first sentence.

The third, and most difficult step, is to figure out how to *show* who the characters are, instead of simply telling. What actions, dialogue, decisions, etc. will show the reader the nature of the character while the character is usually unaware themselves of these aspects of their personality.

The first question is: who are my characters? Do I have a good feel for whom each person is? If you don't, you will find that your characters are two dimensional and not consistent. Your characters must be as true to you as people you know in the real world. The number one thing you must know about every character is: What is their primary motivator?

What do your characters *look like*? You may know, but you will be surprised how many times characters are never really described to the reader. I felt very stupid when I finished a 450 page manuscript and handed it to someone to read and when they finished, they gave it back and said: "Very interesting, but what did your main character look like?"

It is important to describe characters as soon as possible. If you don't, the reader will formulate their own vision of the character and then you can jar them three chapters down the line when you finally get around to describing the character and it doesn't fit the reader's mental vision.

Try to describe characters in such a way that something about each one should stick in the reader's mind. This gets more important, the greater the number of characters you have.

Sometimes, authors choose not to describe their characters because they *want* the reader to think of 'every man' or 'every woman' when they think of each character. That's fine as long as there is a purpose to it.

Character Description

Keep it brief and distinctive. Rather than a long detailed description, focus on one or two things that will stick in the reader's head and makes them think of your character in the way you want them to.

You're not writing a personal ad. Work the information in smoothly, not abruptly.

Use placeholders if it helps. When I collaborated, since we both had to be on the same sheet of music regarding characters, we chose actors and actresses. Not just the actor or actress, but each one in a specific role.

Cliché: Having a character look in a mirror. How many times do we really see ourselves when we look in a mirror? Like any other tool, there are ways around this one. In *Chasing The Ghost* I have my character look in a mirror. But it's more to see the faded picture of his father that he never met which is tucked on one side of the mirror.

You can use other points of view to describe other characters. Rather than simply describing characters, you can describe one character by the reaction of another point of view character. This not only describes that character it gives us some idea of the personality of the POV character based on their perspective.

In the same manner, *names* are very important. You have to decide if you are going to use a character's first name, last name, title (i.e. the doctor, the captain, etc.), or nickname. In your prose use only one name for the same character or else you will confuse the reader.

How does a person get a "handle?" You have the name you were born with. Michael Jay Porter. Then you have what you call yourself. Mike. Then you have what others call you (with or without your liking it.): Mikey, Jay, Port, Bud, Skinny, etc. Then you have your title: Captain, Vice President for Operations, the butcher.

I saw a great cartoon from the Far Side once. It had on the top, *what we call dogs: Fido.* On the bottom it had what dogs call themselves, *I am Fido, terrorizer of the neighborhood, sniffer of trees, master of all that I see.* Or something to that effect. Get the idea?

Given the above two paragraphs, how do you pick names for your characters? The phone book is helpful. Go to the library and wander the stacks and look at author's names. High school and college yearbooks.

You do need to consider that the name fits the character. Many names denote ethnicity. Think about detectives—don't they all have hard sounding names like Magnum PI? That is done deliberately to affect you subconsciously. Also make sure two characters don't have similar names. I try to avoid or even have names that start with the same letter. Unless, of course, you have a specific reason for doing so as Tolkien did by naming the chief wizard, Saruman, who turns out to be a shadow of Sauron.

You should try to stick with one name for each character. Above I mentioned the number of names/titles each of us has. But if you start using all those various names interchangeably throughout a manuscript you can confuse the reader. If you alternate using first name/ last name for your characters you are doubling the number of names the reader has to remember. Try to pick one name and stick with it as much as possible. Of course there will be times when another name/ title comes in, such as in dialogue, but in your prose make it as easy on the reader as you can.

Character Names

Choose a name that fits the character, evokes personality, but doesn't make the reader giggle.

Choose a name that can be read without causing the reader to pause.

In prose, use only one name for each character.

Try to avoid names that begin with the same letter.

So what else do you need to know about a character (I will stay with the female here, no discrimination intended)? The absolute most important thing you have to know about your character is: what is her motivation? Then you also need:

What does she look like? How does she talk? How does she act physically? Any mannerisms?

What is her background? Where was she born? What were her parents like? How was she raised? Where did she go to school? What level education?

What is her job? What special skills does her job require and how will they affect her role in the story? What about hobbies and talents learned from them?

What is her family? Husband? Her relation to him? Children? Relation? Why not kids? Divorced? Why? Why not?

Where is she from? Did she grow up in a city or on a farm?

What secrets does she have?

Some other aspects of a character to keep in mind:

movement

dress

attitudes

gestures

manner

culture

context—class

values and beliefs

needs

motives

dreams

fears

stressors

1st family, which is the family of origin

2d family, which is the present family

The list could go on and on. I highly recommend putting some brainwork into your characters before writing your first page and not make it up as you go along. I say this from my own experience. The review on my second novel from the NY Times said, "The characters are right out of Action Comics." Not very nice, but true. But I learned my lesson after many manuscripts.

On my latest book, *Duty, Honor, Country a Novel of West Point & the Civil War,* I spent an entire month before starting the book working on characters. I invented two fictional families and then developed their entire history, including the family secrets. Spending a month totally vested in the characters made them real to me.

Now, here's something to consider: You can make your characters up out of the blue using the questions (and more) listed above. But you will be more realistic using parts of people that you have met like your mother and father and the loan officer at the bank. This runs you the danger of getting sued, of course. No, no, listen. Look at people you know as character types and use some of their traits but not them as a person. Confusing enough? Try psychology. There are several books on the market that have tests you can take that will define people by type. Get some of these books and use them to help round out your characters. They list out traits of certain personality types. Traits you can use to round out your characters. We'll discuss the Myers-Briggs shortly and that's one way to come up with 16 different character types.

You make believable characters by showing how they react/act in a crisis. "Actions speak louder than words." True. Also remember, though, that the same action done for two different reasons, makes the action seem very different to the reader. Your main character kills someone. Is that bad? It depends, you say. Depends on who they killed. Why they killed them. Under what circumstances.

Remember all those answers. Because eventually you will have to answer them to the reader and they also give you the opportunity to put some twists in your story. For example, character C kills Character J in chapter 3, making C look like a bad egg. But in chapter 7 you reveal that the deceased, J, was in reality a mad scientist about to let loose a plague upon the world and C stopped that by killing him. That certainly changes the reader's perspective on C. A rather dramatic example, I know, but I believe it gets the point across.

You say a lot about your characters by showing what choices they make under pressure, which you make by conflict. I've found that sometimes a person's character totally changes when they are under stress and the "real" person comes out. This can be useful in your plot and storyline especially when your character is in the moment of crisis.

Write up your characters' complete backstory (history), which doesn't necessarily have to be in the book, but you have to know in order to be able to write believable characters. All of your characters have a background prior to the beginning of the novel. Make sure you know it and where applicable, let the reader know parts of it in order to understand the characters better.

Now, the astute reader is saying: "Hey, you're contradicting yourself. Earlier you said to let a character's actions speak for themselves and to try not to get into a character's head to reveal thoughts. How am I going to reveal motive without getting into thoughts?"

Although that is an apparent contradiction, in reality the two are congruous. My question to you is: How do you know anyone's thoughts in day-to-day life other than your own? Through conversation, through watching their actions over a period of time and interpreting, through various means, all short of saying "Jim thought . . ..". Taking it a step further, if you are always in your characters' heads, how can you keep a motive secret, something that might be essential to the suspense of your story?

I also recommend against using quotation marks to delineate a character's thoughts. I see this on occasion in manuscripts and think it is a poor technique for several reasons: First, you confuse the reader who naturally assumes quotation marks mean dialogue. You're making the reader work, and the reader bought your book for enjoyment, not to work. Second, if you are writing third person, how do you draw the line between those thoughts that go inside the quotation marks and everything else in narrative, which to a certain extent is also from a character's point of view? Third, it's telling not showing.

Think of your favorite book. What's the first thing that comes to mind when you bring it up in your brain? I'm willing to bet it's the characters. Most people relate to people, not things.

Characters bring emotion to story, and emotion is what attaches readers to books. It took me a while to truly appreciate this fundamental truth of fiction. I remember meeting Elizabeth George in Denver while she was on book tour about ten years ago. As we dined, she kept talking about characters. How important they are. How characters develop plot, not vice versa.

Here are seven key elements to unforgettable characters.

"Know the enemy and know yourself.

In a hundred battles, you will never be defeated." Sun Tzu. As I teach in *Write It Forward*, before we can understand other people, even fictional ones, we must understand ourselves. So, yes, if you're a writer, you'll need some therapy. It's not normal to sit alone in a dark room and write 100,000 words. You need to understand your point of view on people and things because that's going to come out when you develop your characters. One of the biggest breakthroughs I had on character was when I realized I was writing a character who was doing things I would never in a million years do, but I was able to write him believing he was doing the right thing.

Everyone has a primary motivator.

You must know the primary motivator for every character. Be able to say it in one word. Because when characters are pushed to the limit, that primary motivator is going to determine their course of action, not your decision as author. In *Lonesome Dove*, when Blueduck kidnaps Lori, Larry McMurtry did not have a choice as to what each of this characters were going to do. Because they were fully developed, they all acted 'in character'. Gus went after Lori=loyal. Call kept the cattle moving north=duty. Jake Spoon went to San Antonio and gambled=addiction. In my current WIP, my protagonist's primary motivator is 'loyalty'. My antagonist's primary motivator is 'honor.' Do you see how those two motivators can truly clash and bring the fuel of a novel: conflict?

You need at least three layers of motivation to your main characters.

These layers are all present at the beginning of the book, but the character isn't conscious of the deeper ones. They can be layered thus:

What do you want?
What do you really want?
What do you absolutely need?

Those layers are peeled away until we get down to that need.

In the books Jenny Crusie and I wrote, each peeling away occurred at a turning point in the novel. They are all present at the beginning of the story, they just aren't in the conscious mind. JT Wilder in *Don't Look Down:*

What do you want? Get paid and get laid. (He's a guy.)
What do you really want? A relationship.
What do you need? A relationship *and* community.

You don't have to invent characters from scratch.

If you're not going to use real people (modified), then use what experts have developed for you. I like using variations of three templates, which we'll cover in detail.

Archetypes. This is very useful for gender differences. Is there any male equivalent of slut? That always provokes good debate.

Profiling. I'm big on profiling because it gives you characters types that will act in certain ways. And no, it isn't just for serial killers. You can profile anyone. Indeed, in *Write It Forward*, one exercise participants do is profile themselves first.

The Myers-Briggs. Many of you have taken it, but it gives you 16 distinct character types you can mine. By the way, one type, INFJ, is labeled author. The exact opposite, ESTP, is promoter. Something we focus on in **Write It Forward**.

Know your characters' blind spot.

We use a trait-need-flaw diagram to find that. It's the flaw your character isn't aware of that makes for compelling fiction and is the groundwork of tragedy.

Make your antagonist a real person, not a cardboard cutout.

We must understand WHY the antagonist is doing a bad thing. By the way, evil is not a motivator. It's an end result.

Character Is Pre-Eminent

- Emotion is more important than logic
- Mission or the Men
- Goals are what characters are striving for
- Motivation is why they are striving for their goals

The Anomaly that Intrigues

Your basic story dynamic is the Protagonist (the character who owns the story) struggles with . . .The Antagonist (the character who if removed will cause the conflict and story to collapse) because both must achieve their concrete, specific . . .Goals (the external, concrete things they are each trying desperately to get, not necessarily the same thing).

The Protagonist must be someone the reader wants to identify and spend time with: smart, funny, kind, skilled, interesting, *different*. Consider giving your protagonist an anomaly. What this means is they have something in their character that doesn't seem to 'fit' who they appear to be. Russell Crowe in *LA Confidential* is, in essence, a thug cop used as muscle. No one thinks he's very smart. But from the very beginning of the movie, he goes out of his way to protect women in peril, even when he has no vested interest. Why? That 'why' is a hook that keeps you following his character. This anomaly gets explained eventually.

How do we get a character anomaly out quickly? To give us some examples, let me use some popular TV shows:

A private investigator with OCD. His name is Monk.

A brilliant diagnostic doctor, addicted to vicodin, who hates people but saves their lives. His name is House.

A southern belle in LA, always wears dresses, had an affair in her previous job with her new boss; she heads a major crimes unit in LA and is a superb CLOSER. (Fish out of water story)

I've watched a lot of canceled series on Hulu lately. Some had really good ideas, but the character just didn't cut it:

Life: What if a LA cop is wrongly convicted of murder, sent to prison, but then is exonerated by DNA and as part of his settlement gets 50 million dollars AND his gold detective badge so he can try to find the real murderer.

Good idea. The writing was decent. But the character just didn't pop. Lasted one season. The anomaly they tried to give the character didn't work: he buys a huge mansion with his money, but he doesn't put any furniture in it. Besides not being very interesting, it doesn't make sense.

Standoff: A male-female hostage negotiation team who are secretly having an affair, have it revealed during a situation.

The writing on that show was actually very good. Some excellent episodes. But if your hero and heroine are involved from the pilot, you don't have that Moonlighting or X-Files sexual tension.

Remember to consider extremes when writing about characters in order to involve your reader more intensely. You can have a good character and a bad character. But would the reader prefer to see an evil character and a noble character? Think of personalities as a pendulum and understand that the further you swing that pendulum, the more involved the reader usually will be. Therefore, take any very positive trait you can think of and try to find its opposite. Do the reverse. Then use those traits to develop your characters.

Your protagonist must be in trouble, *usually* not random. What this means is that the problem should occur to your character because of who or what they are, not just because they're in the wrong place at the wrong time. That can only work if the writing is fantastic and the character is unique, but otherwise it's called coincidence.

The protagonist must be introduced as soon as possible, first is preferred. Usually, we must meet the protagonist by the end of the second scene. Right away you're signaling something to the reader if you introduce the problem before the protagonist and vice versa.

Your protagonist must have strong, believable motivation for pursuing her external and specific goal. Note I say external and specific goal—something tangible. Don't confuse goal with motivation.

We often empathize with a reluctant protagonist. Donald Maass in *How To Write The Breakout Novel* says that redemption is the most powerful character arc. The problem is having empathy initially with a character who needs to be redeemed. So we must see the spark of redemption in a negative protagonist very quickly. In the first scene where we meet them, we must see them do something, often a very minor act, sometimes even just one sentence worth, that resonates in the reader's subconscious that the character has the potential for redemption.

There is a clip in the film *Nobody's Fool*, starring Paul Newman that I use to show this when I teach. The basic premise of the movie is Paul Newman's character is a bum, down and out handyman, renting a room upstairs in Jessica Tandy's house. His son has returned to town with his two grandsons and Newman wants a relationship with them. The problem is, when his son was born, Newman abandoned him. So the son is naturally blocking Newman's attempts.

In the clip I use, Jessica Tandy's character calls for Newman to help with an elderly neighbor who is wandering the streets in her dementia. Newman, without putting on his shoes or his jacket goes out into the snowy cold street to help the neighbor. Even though he is not the most likable when it comes to his past, this gives the viewers of the movie reason to believe he is a redeemable character.

The protagonist, as she is at the beginning of the book, would fail if thrust into the climactic scene. This is something you should check after your first draft is done. Take the protagonist from the opening, throw her into the climactic scene, and the bad guy should win. Her arc is the change that allows her to triumph where she wouldn't have before.

The protagonist drives the main storyline story. You have one for one main storyline. You will always have one protagonist and one antagonist. In *Butch Cassidy and the Sundance Kid* who is the protagonist?

Butch.

Why? Because he always comes up with the plans. "You keep thinking Butch; that's what you're good at."

In *Lonesome Dove* who is the protagonist? Even though we might love Gus the most, the protagonist is Call, because he keeps the plot moving via the cattle drive. Also he is the one still standing at the very end, right back where he started from.

Remember that your protagonist is only as good as the antagonist is bad. There would be no Clarice Sterling without a Hannibal Lecter.

If your protagonist fails, what happens? This tells you what is at stake in your story.

The protagonist is the person on stage in the climactic scene, defeating the . . .

The antagonist, who we will cover shortly.

Show, Don't Tell

- Actions speak louder than words. We've all seen people who are saying one thing while doing another. Which do you believe?
- Do your characters react 'naturally'. Given their primary motivator, when faced with a decision, do they go to that motivation even if it turns out to be a bad decision?
- Give the spark of redemption.
- How do your characters react in a crisis? This tells us their true nature.

Goals and Motivation

Your character goals help drive the story because it's what the character is moving toward for the entire book. The goal should be something external and tangible. While they will have many underlying internal goals, the main goal should be clearly stated. Again, much like the Kernel Idea, I recommend you write this down. Your characters goals will help you set up motivation (the why) and the conflict (the why not) and keep the readers invested.

Motivation is the most important factor to consider when having your character make choices or do actions. Once you have a feel for your characters' motivation and they come alive for you, then to a certain extent you lose control over your story. For your characters to be realistic, they have to react like the people you have developed them to be, not like you want them to react in order to move your story ahead. Every time a character acts or reacts, I ask myself if that is consistent with whom I projected the character to be.

For example, in *Atlantis*, I wrote a scene where some people were trying to talk my main character into traveling back to Cambodia where he had last been over thirty years ago. Where his Special Forces team had been wiped out horribly and my character had had nightmares about for years. And I needed my character to agree to go (or else the book would have been rather short). But I had to come up with a legitimate reason for my character to go. I had to figure out what would motivate him to agree to do something that he (or any other sane person) would not do. And it had to be believable to the reader, which means it had to be believable to my character.

Often your protagonist is initially reluctant to get involved and circumstances force him or her to do so. Your protagonist also usually begins by reacting, but eventually must make choices and take actions or else they will lose reader empathy.

Remember to consider extremes when writing about characters in order to involve your reader more intensely. You can have a good character and a bad character. But would the reader prefer to see an evil character and a noble character? Think of personalities as a pendulum and understand that the further you swing that pendulum, the more involved the reader usually will be. Therefore, take any very positive trait you can think of and try to find its opposite. Do the reverse. Then use those traits to develop your characters.

You need to study people and also remember that you were not the original mold for mankind. Some people are very different than you and have different value systems. I think authors who have very good characters understand this, much better than the average person.

I read an interesting thing the other day in a psychology book: the author said that everyone has a religion. What he meant was that everyone has something they believe in, even if it's not to believe in God. To write good characters, you need to know what their value and belief system is, then keep them acting according to that system. Even a crazy serial killer has a belief system, skewed as it may be. In fact, dissecting that belief system is often the task of the novel's protagonist in order to catch the serial killer.

I think you need to adopt a psychological structure for character types. You can invent your own from scratch, but it's easier to use one that already exists and has been thoroughly developed.

A book I recommend reading is John Douglas' *Mindhunter*. Douglas was one of the founders of the FBI's Investigative Support Unit that specialized in profiling. What an author does is actually the opposite of what his unit does. A profiler looks at the evidence then tries to figure who the person is. An author invents the person then needs to come up with the evidence that would be representative of that person. Another interesting aspect of profiling is that it shows that people have character traits that are locked in and that those traits dictate their actions, called habit.

For me, one of the hardest thing to do as a writer is develop an agenda for a character that is something I don't personally have, and then keep in mind that the character is not totally aware of his own agenda and as a writer *show* the reader this agenda. In *Duty, Honor, Country* I had to realistically portray both Union and Confederate characters and show how those on each side truly believed in their cause.

Motivation

Every character thinks the story is about them. Do you know many minions? Many sidekicks? Everyone thinks every situation is about them, so treat all your characters with respect and not as pawns.

Everyone has a core motivation. The thing that will ultimately determine how they act, especially in a crisis.

Victor Frankl called this the 'One Thing'.

The motivation can be anything.

The motivation must be believable to the reader.

What Is Fear?

It is a feeling of alarm or disquiet caused by the expectation of danger, pain, or the like. The reality is that many people's primary motivator is fear. However, they cloak the fear with other terms, such as security. You must figure out what each of your characters are afraid of. For your protagonist, he/she must ultimately face down some fear, even if it's not central to the story. Indiana Jones hates— snakes. What did it have to be? Snakes.

Heroism is taking action in the face of fear. If a character has no fear then he/she is a socio/psychopath. While these people do exist, most of your characters will have fear on some level. To be heroic is to act in the face of that fear and this helps bind the reader to the character.

Fear is an emotion. It can not be thought away. It also serves some positive purposes.

It often stems from uncertainty. This is a good way to involve the reader in your story. If the reader starts to become afraid for the fate of your characters, then you've involved them in the story.

It is often the primary motivator for people as we require base needs to be fulfilled first, if we look at . . .

Maslow's Hierarchy Of Needs
Self-Actualization

Esteem—something outside of ourselves that we believe in.

Belongingness and Love—we need people around us and to have a connection with them.

Safety Needs—a place to live; being safe from your environment.

Physiological Needs—taking care of basic survival needs like food, water and air.

Remember, your characters are not all self-actualized. They are usually somewhere in the middle of Maslow's hierarchy. Often, your protagonist's arc is to tear them down the hierarchy and then build back up.

CHARACTER EXERCISE: *Where on Maslow's hierarchy is your protagonist at the beginning of the book? Then end?*

Where on Maslow's hierarchy is your antagonist at the beginning of the book? At the end?

Blind Spot

Needs produce blind spots

Everyone has blind spots

As an author, make sure you know yours

Strongest defenses are built around the blind spot. Therefore . . .

Often the blind spot is the part of character thought to be the strongest

Denial defends blinds spot and justifies needs

Blind spots are the making of tragedy

To find blind spots, use the triangle of personality traits: Trait, Need, Flaw. The flaw is the potential blind spot, because any character trait pushed to an extreme becomes a negative. Here are examples:

Trait	Need	Flaw
Loyal	To be trusted	Gullible
Adventurous	To have change	Unreliable
Altruistic	To be loved	Submissive
Tolerant	To have no conflict	No conviction
Decisive	To be in charge	Impetuous
Realistic	To be balanced	Outer control
Competitive	To achieve goals	Overlook cost
Idealistic	To be the best	Naive

I could go on and on with this list, but when developing your character's traits, also fill in the need that drives them and the flaw that brings them to their darkest moment. Usually, the flaw is a blind spot for the character; i.e. the character is not aware of the flaw.

CHARACTER EXERCISE: *What is your protagonist's blind spot? What is your antagonist's blind spot?*

Good Characters Should Be:

Heroic: They struggle to meet every day challenges or extreme challenges. Either way they show courage and dignity in their battle. They don't have to be nice, but they do have to be good. If you start with a negative character there must be a glimmer of hope the reader can discern that they could change for the better.

Believable: Give them strengths *and* weaknesses. Often it is the latter that readers identify with more. And you must give consistent evidence of these traits, not just show it once.

Sympathetic: Readers like characters who make things happen; who actively respond to the world around them instead of constantly reacting. Readers don't particularly care for victims. Remember I said above that you get to truly know someone by how they react in a crisis—in the same manner, characters grab our attention when they face a crisis. Also remember that opposing external traits cause inner conflict.

Memorable: Think back about your favorite book and what do you remember? The characters.

Sometimes *less is better.* What I mean is that occasionally I'll get a manuscript to read and as soon as the main character is introduced, we get their entire life history. How do you feel about meeting someone like that in real life, where you know everything about them at the first meeting? What's the point in seeing them again?

You, as the author, have to know everything about your character, but you don't have to tell the reader everything. A little mystery is intriguing. You know how your character developed a quirky trait, but by not telling the reader up front, you make the reader curious. For example, in the movie *LA Confidential*, we meet each of the three main characters in three opening scenes and each of them shows us something about who they are by actions they take, but we don't know *why* they're taking those actions until much further in the movie. Wanting to know that why keeps the reader hooked.

The best way to think about your characters is as if they were real people your readers are meeting for the first time on a blind date. Make the meeting a memorable one and make the character someone the reader wants to go out with again.

Developing Characters and Character Templates

Characters must *feel* real to both the writer and the reader. How do you create a realistic character? You base your characters on what you already know about people. When developing your characters consider the following:

Where do your characters come from? As part of your process, you must have a consistent way of developing fully rounded characters.

Invented or real life. Are you going to invent your characters or assemble them from people you know?

How does the reader meet them? As in real life, that first meeting is key.

How do you get to know people? That's the same way readers get to know your characters.

What happens in their first scene?

What is the key point in their life?

Domino theory—did they have a key event in their past that shaped them forever?

What is their motivation?
You have to know everything about your character.
The reader doesn't.
Less is better.

Types Of Characters

The *protagonist* is the person you are writing about. They **own** the story and drive the main story line. You have only one protagonist. Your other characters support the main character and main plot.

Types of protagonists

Reluctant protagonists
Empathetic protagonists
Negative protagonists

A *reluctant protagonist* is generally an ordinary character who is thrust into extraordinary situations. Bruce Willis in *Die Hard* is a reluctant protagonist. This type of character could also be a person with extraordinary abilities, but has no desire or wishes not to use these powers. *X-Men* is an example of this type of character.

The *empathetic protagonist* invokes a feeling of empathy in the reader toward the main character. The reader is heavily invested in the goals of this character because they feel some connection with them. Often, the reluctant protagonist is an empathetic one as well.

The *negative protagonist,* also known as the *antihero,* can be the most fun, but can also be the most difficult to write. The negative protagonist must have some redeeming quality in order for the reader to want to spend their time with him. The hit HBO series, *Dexter*, is a good example of a negative protagonist. He is a blood splatter analysis expert for the Miami PD who moonlights as a serial killer. Not very likable sort of fellow. But here is what makes him empathetic...he only kills other very bad people.

Your protagonist might be a combination of the above. The key is to understand their core personality and how you want the reader to emotionally connect with them.

When developing your protagonist ask yourself what would happen if they failed. This will help you set up your climactic scene, which is what the entire book is driving toward. It will also help lay the foundation for character arc. And it tells you what's at stake in your story.

Take your protagonist as you know them in the beginning of the book and dump them into the climactic scene. That character should fail because they have not changed. The arc of the story changes them so that when the climactic scene comes, they are now a person capable of defeating the protagonist.

Antagonist

The *antagonist* is the character that is causing your protagonist's conflict. The antagonist drives the plot initially by introducing the problem. If you remove this character, the plot will collapse.

It is just as important for you to know goals and motivation of your antagonist. What is his/her plan? In order to understand how the conflict will play out and to draw believable characters you must give the same diligence to developing the antagonist as you do the protagonist. The stronger the antagonist the stronger your protagonist will be.

Evil is not a motivation. It's the result of motivation, which is something much deeper.

Characters In Conflict

Conflict is rooted in different motivations, even if they want the same thing

Three levels to motivation
Inner—the character's own inner turmoil.
Personal—between characters.
Universal—the character battling the world around them and fate.

Fear is often a primary motivator

Often your protagonist must overcome fear, even if it isn't their primary motivator

Character And Community

Your main character is part of a larger cast that consists of a community. A sense of belonging is part of human nature. In order to create characters that come alive in the minds of the reader we have to develop secondary characters. Most people want a sense of community and often it forms around the main character. Community can also give you great latitude in tone, pacing, POV.

Kinds Of Community

Ensemble casts, where different characters fill different roles. For example, in *Don't Look Down*, a lot of the humor came from supporting characters, not the hero or heroine.

Disposable characters. It's a great dramatic tool to kill off a major character.

Buddy stories. Think of *Lethal Weapon*. Mixing two different types of characters can set up great tension. Also, readers often like a community around your protagonist.

Character Templates

Why reinvent the wheel? There's no reason to invent characters from scratch. You can use real people to lay the foundation for your characters.

Or you can use what the experts have already done for you:

Profiling
Archetypes
Myers-Briggs

Profiling

I mentioned profiling under goals and motivation when I recommended the book *Mindhunter* by John Douglas based on the FBI Behavioral Science Unit which tracks serial killers.

You can profile anyone and I recommend you start with yourself. Understand that 99% of what we do is habit. The habitual things we do equal our behavior patterns. Start with the end result of a behavior pattern, and work backwards to start profiling yourself and others.

Many people confuse CSI and Profilers. The basic difference is that CSI looks for *specific* clues that point to a *specific* person. A profiler looks for *patterns* pointing to a *type* of person.

CHARACTER EXERCISE: *What is your protagonist's profile for a normal day? What is your antagonist's profile for a normal day? What is your profile for your normal day as a writer?*

Archetypes

Another way to develop characters is through typical Archetypes and Gender differences.

Female	Male
Boss	Chief
Seductress	Bad-boy
Spunky-kid	Best-friend
Free-spirit	Charmer
Waif	Lost-soul
Librarian	Professor
Crusader	Swashbuckler
Nurturer	Warrior

Caveat. Be careful when using archetypes. They are an oversimplification of personality and often times cliché. They are great for laying the foundation of the kind of characters you will create. You're job from there is to make them real and unique.

In the above title there are some interesting things to note. The top left B term isn't the one often used. The bottom pairing is unique. This is why we were taught if we kicked a door and there were two terrorists inside the room, a male and a female, we shot the woman first. Women tend to be more black or white than men. If you talk to school teachers: if two boys are fighting, you can break them up. But if two girls are fighting, you probably need to get help. Men do not often boil a woman's rabbit.

Archetypes are useful to understand that the same motivations in a man and a woman can result in a different type of person.

Myers-Briggs

The Myers-Briggs was developed in 1943. It is not a test, but an indicator personality inventory, so there are no 'right' or 'wrong' labels. The idea behind Myers-Briggs is that what seems to be a random variation in behavior is really consistent behavior depending on where any given individual falls in each type.

There are four main areas with two possible orientations to each personality, which equals 16 character 'types'.

However, the actual test is a sliding scale. The best place to start is with yourself. So look at the following areas and figure out where you fall. Understanding yourself will help you apply this type of character development in your own writing.

CHARACTER EXERCISE: *Where do your characters fall in each of these categories?*

Area One	
Block A	**Block B**
Act first, think later?	Think first, then act?
Feel deprived if cut off from interacting with the outside world?	Require private time to get energized?
Tend to be motivated by the outside world?	Tend to be internally motivated?
Get energized by groups?	Groups drain your energy?

Area Two	
Block A	**Block B**
Mentally live in the now?	Mentally live in the future?
Use common sense for practical solutions?	Use imagination for innovative solutions?
Your memory focuses on detail and facts?	Your memory focuses on patterns and context?
Don't like guessing?	Comfortable with guessing?

Area Three	
Block A	**Block B**
Search for facts when making a decision?	Focus on feelings when making a decision
Notice work to be accomplished?	Focus on people's needs?
Tend to provide an objective analysis	Seek consensus and popular opinions?
Believe conflict is normal part of relationships?	Dislike conflict and avoid it if at all possible?

Area Four	
Block A	**Block B**
Plan detail before taking action?	Are comfortable moving into action without a plan?
Focus on tasks and complete them in order?	Like to multitask and can mix work with play?
Keep ahead of deadlines to avoid stress and work optimally?	Work best closer to deadlines?
Set targets, dates?	Avoid commitments that might interfere with your freedom?

Results	
1A= Extrovert (E)	1B= Introvert (I)
2A= Sensing (S)	2B= Intuition (N)
3A= Thinking (T)	3C= Feeling (F)
4A= Judging (J)	4B= Perceiving (P)

Myers-Brings Types	
INTP= Architect	ESJF= Seller
ENTP= Inventor	ISFJ= Conservator
INTJ= Scientist	ESFP= Entertainer
ENTJ= Field Marshall	ISFP= Artist
INFP= Quester	ESTJ= Administrator
ENFP= Journalist	ISTJ= Trustee
INFJ= Author	ESTP= Promoter
ENJF= Pedagogue	ISTP= Artisan

Extroversion vs. Introversion

This is how we view the world

Extroverts are social

Introverts are territorial

Extroverts prefer breadth and a wide variety of personal communications. Introverts prefer depth and one on one

Extroverts tend to be externally motivated. Introverts tend to be internally motivated

75% Extroverts 25% Introverts

Intuition vs. Sensation

Innovative vs. Practical

This is how we think

This is the greatest source of misunderstanding between people

25% Intuitive   75% Sensation

Thinking vs. Feeling

The thinking part of our brain analyzes and decides in a detached manner

The feeling part of our brain analyzes and decides in an attached manner

Impersonal vs. personal

This is how we make decisions and act

Logic vs. emotion

50% Thinking 50% Feeling but . . .

More men are Thinking and more women are Feeling

Judging vs. Perceiving

Closure vs. Open-ended

This is how we approach our endeavors

Results or process

50% Judging 50% Perceiving

As you develop your characters, place them inside the four main areas and figure out their personality type and then you can begin to shape them into real three-dimensional characters that really pop off the page.

Character Change and Arc

Earlier we discussed putting our protagonist in the climactic scene as they are in the beginning of the book. In order to have a fully developed character, they must change. Change is what produces character arc. The key to character arc is to show the change, not tell it.

Change requires three things to happen

Moment Of Enlightenment
Experience something never experienced before.

Experience something you've experienced before, but it affects you differently than ever before. This is the classic 'light bulb going on'.

By itself, it is not change, just a momentary awareness.

Decision
Because of the Moment of Enlightenment, a decision is made.

It is not necessarily a good decision.

Character is then a) Stuck with the decision (externally imposed change) or

b) Sticks with the decision (internally motivated change)

By itself, a decision is not change, just a fleeting commitment.

Sustained Action
Because of the decision, behavior is changed.

The changed behavior is sustained long enough to become habit.

In the military, this is called training.

The 5% rule for external and internal sustained action. I explain this in detail in *Write It Forward*, but essentially 5% of people are capable of internally motivated change.

Sustained action leads to change.

CHARACTER EXERCISE

What is your protagonist's moment of enlightenment?

What decision does your protagonist make because of that?

What sustained action does your protagonist do that produces change?

The Resolution & Character Arc

By the end of the book we want to know our protagonist has changed.

We need to see them do something emotional they weren't capable of doing at the beginning of the book. Often they are in a similar situation as earlier in the story, but this time they make the opposite decision.

This completes the character arc that is the core of your book.

Use Other Fictional Characters

This isn't plagiarism. It's like using real people: you just change the details. It's giving you a template. In my book *Duty, Honor, Country*, one of the things I started with was a story concept such as the one the HBO mini-series *Rome* used: two fictional characters set against a historical setting. We know what happened historically, we just aren't certain *why* many things happened. I've taken two West Points cadets and back-dropped them against the events going from 1840 to the climax of the battle of Shiloh. I'm using the same types of characters, not the characters themselves.

Beyond that, though, I hit a speed bump about 85,000 words into the book. I was liking my secondary character a lot better than my protagonist. And that was bothering me. Until I remembered that in my favorite book of all time, *Lonesome Dove*, Gus is a much more likable and empathetic character than Call. Yet Call is the protagonist because he drives the plot. This allowed me to relax and put my characters back into focus.

Character bottom line

Before you begin writing, spend some time getting to know your characters. The more real they are to you, the more real they will be on the page and to readers.

Tool 6: Idea Into Story: Plot

Plot

A story is a character trying to resolve a problem.

I use to say a story was a problem that needed to be resolved. Using *Write It Forward,* I now see my blind spot. I was leaving out the part of writing that I was weakest at in my definition of plot: character.

A plot is a series of events that outline the action of a story. Notice it says action. Things have to happen.

The characters' motivations drive the plot toward the climax. The number one thing you must know about every character is their primary motivator.

Time is linear. Usually. We'll discuss time in more detail later. I realized I had to do a twelve year time jump in *Duty, Honor, Country.* I was struggling for weeks on how to cover those twelve years. Every solution I came up with had either too much detail or not enough. I couldn't find the balance until I went to my Beta Reader and asked for help. I gave each of the six main characters a single important historical scene in those years that showed whether the character was changing or staying the same, so that by the time we resume a normal timeline in the Civil War, the reader isn't jarred by the characters when they meet again.

Plot: By Aristotle
An interesting character facing a problem

Story is solving the problem

Tragedy: In solving the problem, it gets worse, which leads to the dark moment, which leads to the turning point

Character must plausibly solve the problem

There are six good questions to ask yourself before you begin writing:

What do I want to write about?

What do I want to say about it?

Why do I want to say it?

Why should anybody else care?

What can I do to make them care?

What do I want readers to do, think or see?

What I have found is that most writers can answer the first three, but not the last three. The last three focus on the reader, while the first three on the writer.

The longer I write, the more I write like a reader, rather than a writer. That might sound strange, but as I write, I put myself in the position of the reader. Have I hooked the reader? Am I maintaining suspense? What does the reader know up to this point? Remember, you're trying to get a story that's inside your head, into the reader's head. I try to constantly be aware of what I've developed in the reader's head.

The key to all the techniques and tools is that they must be used to insure *smoothness*. By smoothness, I mean that your writing must not jar the reader either in term of style or story. The reader is interested in the story. Reading is the means by which they learn the story, but it is only a medium. The medium must not get in the way of the story. When the reader is pulled out of the story into the writing because you didn't use the proper technique, or didn't use it correctly, you stray away from the story.

A good maxim to keep in mind is: "Don't let them know you're writing."

Backstory

Backstory is everything that happens **before** you start your story. You need to know it, but the question is how much does the reader need to know? And when?

The key is to not info dump. The moment you pause the story and start explaining what happened, you're giving too much backstory. It's hard for the writer to see this during draft, so don't worry too much about it until you are in rewrite stages and working on tightening down story. Remember the reader is interested in what is happening now, not what happened ten years ago, even if it is part of the story, it needs to be weaved in only when the reader must know it in order for the story to make sense.

Narrative Structure

Narrative structure can be used as a frame for your outline. I use the template of the five elements of narrative structure.

Inciting Incident
Escalating Conflict
Crisis
Climax
Resolution

Inciting Incident

This is a dynamic event and should be seen by the reader. It upsets the balance of forces and the rest of the novel is an attempt by your protagonist to restore the balance or change things for the better. Often the inciting incident is brought about by the antagonist. A good way to twist the inciting incident is to have what appears to be a good thing turn out to be the worst thing that could possibly happen. We've all heard stories of someone winning the lottery and it ended up ruining their life.

Your opening scene is going to do one of two things: introduce the problem or introduce the protagonist. When you make this decision, right away you are signaling to the reader which you believe to be more important. You could start with the protagonist in the problem, but both have backstory and it could be overwhelming to the reader to get that all at once.

Whichever one you open with, generally the next scene introduces the other. Thus, by the end of the second scene, the reader should know who the protagonist is and what is the problem that needs to be resolved. Don't be a secret keeper—withhold the plot from the reader thinking this engages them. This just upsets readers.

The initiating event is where things change, the fights starts, the balance has been upset. You definitely need a hook within the first few pages of your book. Something that engages the readers emotions and gets them excited to go on the ride that is your story.

If you have a flashback or memory in your opening scene, perhaps you need to rip that out and put it in normal time sequence and make it the opening scene? After all, it's so important, that you need to toss it in there so quickly, maybe by itself it would be a great opening?

One lesson I learned writing thrillers was to introduce the protagonist *before* they become aware of the problem. In a thriller, since the plot stakes are so high, you usually introduce the problem first. Then we go to the protagonist. What you want to do is give a brief view into the protagonist's 'normal' life before they become aware there is this big problem. This is key because it 'sets' the core personality of that character in the reader's mind. It's a small, but important thing.

For example, in *Peacemaker*, the story starts with the problem: ten nuclear warheads are stolen, one is detonated to cover the bad guy's trail. As that one goes off in red flame, we suddenly shift to blue water. The protagonist, Nicole Kidman is swimming laps. We get about ten seconds of that, then a Marine is standing at the side of the pool telling her 'we have a problem'. What does that brief glimpse of her swimming laps tell us about her? She's used to things being in order. She doesn't like chaos. And she's about to be thrust into chaos.

In *Stargate*, the story starts with the Stargate being found. Then we shift to the protagonist Kurt Russell, sitting in a young boy's bedroom holding a gun in his hand. We find out that his son found his gun and accidently shot himself with it. This tells us Russell has nothing to live for. When he goes through the Stargate with that nuke, if necessary, he will detonate it and close the gate. Here's an interesting question: did they pick Russell because of his skills as a commando, or because they knew about his son's death and that he was the perfect person to send on what could be a one-way mission?

Why now? What's changed? Why is the story starting today and not yesterday? You must know the answers to these questions. You can't just randomly pick a start point. There must be a reason why the initiating even is the key moment.

Your opening shot/sentence is key. It's often used to set mood and tone for the story. "It was a dark and stormy night" is a cliché, but clichés are truisms. Start focusing on what the first thing you see on film in a movie is—the first shot. I use the example of the large American flag in *Patton*. As soon it appears most people in the audience know exactly what movie it is even before seeing George C. Scott appear on stage. In the same way, do you remember the first opening shot of the movie *Saving Private Ryan*? Again, it's the American flag, flapping in the wind at the top of the flagpole above the cemetery at Normandy. This tells you the tone of the movie.

Your opening scene often mirrors the climactic scene, except at a lower level. For example, in the movie *Elizabeth*, in the opening scene we see prisoners getting their hair cut off in prison prior to being burned at the stake. The climactic scene is Elizabeth cutting off her hair to become the virgin Queen.

Sometimes, your opening scene can actually be the protagonist and antagonist in conflict and the antagonist wins, normally at a much lower level than in the climactic scene. In the movie *Broken Arrow*, Christian Slater and John Travolta are boxing. John Travolta wins. The climactic scene, they're battling over a nuclear weapon and Slater wins. They use the symbol of a $20 bill which John Travolta wins after the boxing match and then it's floating in the air, singed, after Christian Slater defeats John Travolta at the end.

Something else I've noticed in both books and movies: the larger the story, the smaller the opening and the smaller the story, the larger the opening. It's not a rule, but something to consider. For example, *Dune*, by Frank Herbert is a huge story. There's an entire new universe to explore. But Herbert starts small and doesn't overwhelm the reader. He wants to hook you in to character and the potential of story. So it starts with the protagonist sitting alone in his room in his castle. His mother comes in with a Mother Superior of her order. The Mother Superior tells Paul to put his hand in a hole in a box. She then places a needle against his neck. She tells him that if he removes his hand from the box, she will inject him with the poison in the needle and he'll die like the animal he is. Then his hand begins to feel as if it's on fire. He doesn't take his hand out, even as the pain increases. Finally the Mother Superior turns the box off, turns to the mother and says "He's the one."

The one what? Don't you want to know? But Herbert only slowly introduces us to this new universe and only when absolutely needed. We don't learn about space travel until Paul is getting on a spaceship.

In the opposite way, *The Day of the Jackal*, is a pretty small story. Will the detective catch the Jackal before he kills? But it starts big: Paris early morning. We pan in over Paris until we get into a court-yard with a stake set in the ground. A French officer is led out, tied to the stake and executed by firing squad. We then find out why.

People question whether prologues can be used. Of course they can, but you must make sure you absolutely need one. The only thing that makes a chapter a prologue is that it's out of time sequence with the rest of the book. Often prologues are used in thrillers when the problem occurs well before the start of the story.

Escalating Conflict

The conflict escalates for both the protagonist and the antagonist. People tend to forget that the antagonist's brilliant plan is now falling apart. The Nazgul did not get the ring in the Shire. Now it's in Rivendell. Oops.

Escalating conflict is a series of progressive complications that ups the stakes. As we peel away layers, the stakes for the characters get higher. One way to look at escalating conflict is through the use of Turning Points.

Turning points happen on two levels, internal and external. By focusing on these parts of your story when mapping out narrative structure it will help you keep things simple and focused on the main story line. A turning point is where both the plot and the character arc turn in a new direction, usually with higher stakes.

The stakes get higher, the suspense rises, and the pace of the story gets faster. While the reader actually still reads at the same pace, the book feels like it's getting faster. If you consider a four act structure with three turning points, you're looking at the first act being around 34,000 words or so; the second around 28,000; the third around 22,000 and then the fourth act being around 16,000 or so. Those are just rough figures, but the book picks up pace as the reader moves on.

Surprise is not suspense. Because the reader doesn't know the surprise is coming. So even if you have a surprise (which is hard to pull off), you still need suspense.

Suspense comes from caring about character. Once we get involved with your characters, we care about their fate. We care what happens to them. That is why you have to get us into the characters quickly.

An example of this and use of an opening: Long shot: two lane highway in the middle of west Texas. Four boys sitting on lawn chairs in the middle of the highway drinking cokes. What does that tell us? Not much happening in *Dancer, Texas Pop 81*. The initiating event sort of happened two years prior to today, when the four boys are graduating high school later in the day. When they were sophomores they all went to the bus station and bought tickets to Los Angeles for the Monday after graduation. So they graduate and we follow the four boys through their weekend. We start rooting for this one to stay, and this one to go. On Monday morning, the bus shows up and two get on and two stay. The suspense comes from caring about who stays and who goes.

Make everything serve multiple purposes to tighten the story down.

Crisis

The darkest moment, when it looks as if all is lost. It's usually a fight or flee situation for the protagonist.

You have many minor moments of crisis in your novel, but a single main one. It's when the protagonist's back is against the wall. The protagonist reaches the point where she has to make a decision: fight or flee. The decision leads to a course of action and it shouldn't be an obvious choice, even though we know the protagonist will fight. Still, it has to seem that perhaps, if they were 'smart', they'd flee.

What you must do is give the protagonist a believable motivation to fight. In *Don't Look Down*, Jenny and I sent our first draft in to our editor. She liked it, but also said that on page 254 the hero and heroine, if they were smart, would pack their bags and go home. There was no reason for them to hang around and fight the antagonist. We had to rewrite and add in a compelling motivation for them to take on the antagonist and see the conflict through to the climax.

That choice drives the protagonist toward the inevitable collision with the antagonist in the climax.

PLOT EXERCISE: *What is your moment of crisis for your protagonist? Is it a fight or flee situation?*

Climax

The choice comes to a conclusion.

It's the Protagonist versus the Antagonist and one wins and one loses. Both are on stage. No proxies. Don't have the police racing in at the last minute to arrest the bad guy, unless the police officer is your protagonist.

The climax is the solution to the problem introduced in the inciting incident.

You only get one climactic scene. No matter how neat and kinky it sounds, you don't get a bifurcating climax, which means two climactic scenes. You get one. Because you have one main storyline. Everything else is subplots and you close out your subplots before the climax, usually in reverse order in which they were introduced: Subplots 1, 2, 3, 4, get closed out 4, 3, 2, 1.

The climactic scene is often the same or a mirror image of the opening scene, just at lower level. The protagonist has changed from who she was in the opening scene to the point where she can win. If you took your protagonist as she is at the beginning of the book and plunked her down in the climactic scene, she would lose. This is why, as soon as you finish reading a book, go back and re-read the opening chapter. Look for all the things you didn't consciously notice the first time you read it. Also, think about the protagonist as you meet her and imagine her in the climactic scene.

The end is the solution to the problem that you introduced in one of the first two chapters. But remember all that expository information that you worked into your story? You must also close out all your subplots by the end, which sometimes can be quite difficult to do.

Study endings as much as you study beginnings. How did the author explain all the hidden details that bring the conclusion together? How many chapters did the author write after the climactic scene (hopefully one)?

The *end* line on the diagram is not as flexible as the "beginning" line. When the end comes in your story it comes. Because you have all those pages prior, you have lost a large degree of control over your ending. It should be a *natural* conclusion of the story itself. Sometimes I'm asked how long a manuscript should be and I always say long enough to reach the end.

I believe it is important that you have an idea what the climax of your book is going to be before you start writing it, as that is where the story is driving toward. Some writers don't want to do that—you have to find what works for you.

I think we have all read books where the ending rang flat or disappointed us. The question you should have asked yourself, as a writer is *why* did that ending disappoint? A book should have a pay off for the reader which comes in the resolution, which we'll discuss shortly.

Some writers work from their ending backwards. By this, I mean they know in their mind how they want the story to end and they write the entire book with that in mind.

I think you should have a good idea of your ending when you start writing because if you don't, your writing may tend to wander. It all goes back to outlining and whatever you feel comfortable with. Another problem with not having an idea of your ending is that if your plot is complex you might not conclude with an ending at all as everything simply unravels—or, more likely, you can't tie together all the loose threads to end the book succinctly and in a satisfactory manner.

Stephen King says he doesn't have a clue what his ending is when he starts a book, but I think he is the exception rather than the rule. And he's Stephen King. And recently he's changed that opinion.

The most important thing about the ending is to close out your main storyline and all your subplots. Don't leave the reader guessing.

The climax ends the crisis.

Out of the climax, comes the resolution.

Resolution

The resolution is the pay off for the reader. This should be one, short scene.

Don't leave any loose ends dangling. The reader cares about all the characters and events. You actually tie up your sub-plots before the climactic scene, usually in reverse order to the way they were introduced.

The resolution is the satisfying ending you promised the reader when you introduced the inciting incident. That balance has been restored and the protagonist has changed. Or we are introduced to a new reality.

We have to see the change in our protagonist. They must do something in the last scene that they wouldn't have done at the beginning of the book. For example, in the movie *The Verdict*, Paul Newman was seduced and betrayed by Charlotte Rampling. The final scene is Newman in his law office, after having won the greatest case of his career. Every other time he was in his office he was drinking a beer. But now he's drinking a cup of coffee. He's different. The phone rings. It's Rampling. He knows it's her. He reaches for the phone, but forces his hand to stop. The phone keeps ringing. And ringing. And ringing. Fade to black, roll credits.

The key is that he didn't answer the phone. Who he had been, he would have answered.

He changed.

PLOT EXERCISE: *How is your protagonist different at the end of your book? How do you show this difference?*

Fate vs. Coincidence

I used to believe you can't have coincidence in plot. I called it author manipulation of the plot. I still think you have to be careful. A 'coincidence' has to be handled really well. But there is such a thing as fate. For example, in *Duty, Honor, Country*, I have the inciting incident be a cadet, Cord, getting challenged to a dual for getting the tavern keep's daughter pregnant. My protagonist, Rumble, (not Cord) steps up and asks for the daughter's hand in marriage, thus losing his cadetship.

Cut to the birth six month's later. Rumble is with his wife as she's in labor. U.S. Grant, Longstreet, etc. are with him. Cord, who is persona non grata now, is standing in the tree line about the cabin, waiting. That night, of all nights, I have the proxy of the antagonist ride up, bearing a message for Rumble.

Now in the big scheme of things, that seems a mighty big coincidence. Two years ago I would have not done that. But you know what? Why not that night? If I can keep the emotions of the two conflicts (the birth, the proxy vs. Cord) ramped up and emotional enough, why not? Why have the proxy show up two nights later?

The key to this is fate is layered on top of existing conflict. Coincidence is when the event is the conflict. Then it's author manipulation of the plot. In the example above, the girl is giving birth—that's the core conflict of the scene. The proxy riding up is layered on top of that.

Flashbacks And Memories

The two are not the same. If you've been divorced you know this. A flashback is what happened. A memory is what someone remembers happening. Memory is tainted and slanted by all that happened afterward and by what someone wants now. Entire stories revolve around different memories of the same event, such as *Courage Under Fire* where the protagonist gets everyone's story of what happened in the desert, but only one version is the true version.

You can use both, but use them sparingly because the reader usually wants to know what happens next, not what already happened.

And often there is no conflict in the flashback or memory because they already happened.

The real key to both is that you keep the reader oriented. The reader must know when they enter a flashback/memory and leave, very clearly. Much like your cuts in point of view.

Tightening Story and Chekhov's Gun

A novel is similar to a bunch of strings woven together to make a rope. The tighter the strings (subplots) are woven to each other and to the center storyline, the stronger the rope (story) is. Also, you've got to make sure all the strings (subplots) end inside of that rope (story) to make it a strong one.

Chekov once said: "Don't have a gun in Act One unless you fire it by Act Three." This is true of writing. Don't throw superfluous things into your story. The reader doesn't know the significance of whatever you write so he assumes that *everything* is significant. You disappoint your reader if you have a scene that appears to be important, but you never refer back to it, and wrote it only to keep your action moving.

I amend Chekov's rule though: Don't have a gun unless you *use* it by act three. A really good writer will use the gun again, but not by firing it. They'll use it in some unique manner.

I have often been misled when reading manuscripts for critique because I misjudge the importance of something in early chapters that is never mentioned again. In one case a writer had a large explosion occurring that destroyed quite a bit of property and killed many people. I assumed that this explosion was tied into the main plot; in fact, I figured that the bad guys had caused the explosion. Yet the explosion was never mentioned again nor really explained. The author had simply used it to set up the circumstances causing the hero to have to use a different escape route. It totally threw me off the original story for more than fifty pages as I kept anticipating a reference back to that explosion. That's a story that's not tight.

In the process of writing a book, look at everything that you write with an open mind and something minor can later turn out to be rather important. I call this planting subconscious seeds in your story. This is why you shouldn't edit yourself to death. You might put something in your story that doesn't seem significant, yet ends up being critical.

For example, in *Agnes and the Hitman*, we located Two Rivers, Agnes' house on a point of land where a river intersects with the Intracoastal Waterway. We also put a tidal cut across the point of land, which at high tide, essentially makes Agnes' house an island. An old wooden bridge is part of her driveway.

I'm not sure why we did this initially. But here's how it tightened down over the drafts:

1) The isolation of her land and the tidal cut reflected the way her life was isolated at the beginning of the story.

2)The old bridge that creaked ominously every time a car went over it reflected the overall state of her house. Agnes worried every time a car went over it, reflecting her worry about being able to pull off the wedding at Two Rivers.

3) The antagonist ends up attacking someone and they end up in the cut next to the bridge.

4) The antagonist ends up attacking the bridge to try to stop the wedding.

5) My hero ends up replacing the bridge for her in a rather, um, phallic way (you have to read the book) that brings the hero and heroine closer together.

Thus, a simple piece of setting, a bridge, and serves at least five purposes in the book. We didn't think of all of those at once. They developed as we rewrote. Ultimately, the bridge represents connection between Agnes and the world.

I think this is an example of the power of the subconscious. You write three ways to tighten a story down and in this case we:

Knew from the very beginning that the bridge would be a symbol of connection.

We added in events at the bridge as the plot developed and we found it to be central to certain parts of the action.

We went back and rewrote things about the bridge to tighten the plot down.

The example I use for this is in Pat Conroy's classic *The Lords of Discipline.* Far into the story the protagonist is in a bind. He must discover the identities of a secret group called The Ten. Earlier in the book, there's a scene where he's in the study of his roommate's father. Pat Conroy described the study, noting the leather-bound notebooks on a shelf which the roommate had told him were his father's memoirs which no one was allowed to read.

The protagonist discovers that the father was a member of The Ten when he was a cadet, so he figures the way to discover the current Ten is break in the study and read the journals.

The question is: Did Pat Conroy know that was the solution to the problem from the very start and thus, when writing the earlier scene in the study, he knew ahead of time the importance of those journals?

Or perhaps Conroy didn't know the importance of those journals as the solution to the later problem and put them in there just to say something about the father? And then when the protagonist was stuck, Conroy was just as stuck. But looking back through what he'd written, much as the protagonist would look back on what he had experienced, he suddenly realized: The Journals! Perhaps, originally Conroy just put those journals in there as part of character development. But suddenly realizes he can use them in another way.

Or perhaps there were no journals in that study. Conroy was in the same bind as his protagonist. But being the master of the story, Conroy went back and inserted the journals as a solution to the problem. The issue with this, though, is that now Conroy has to rewrite the entire book with those journals in there. It might change minor things or it might change major things.

All three paths are ones you will use as a writer.

Every character, incident, location—everything—you put into your novel has to be examined very carefully. What additional use can you make of it? The more uses you can make of each subplot, the tighter the story. The tighter the story, the better the manuscript.

▪ ▪ ▪
Tool 7: The Parts

Dialogue

It's important to remember that psychologists say that a very large percentage of communication is nonverbal, yet on the printed page all you have are the words. There is no tone, no facial expressions, no hand gestures, nothing that in normal face-to-face communication can drastically affect the message being communicated. Because all you have are the words, you must choose them very carefully. A conversation in a novel is *not* exactly as it would be in "real life". Because you are lacking the things you would have in real life, you make up for it with your word choice. You also must be aware that you can't bore the reader, thus your written dialogue is usually more concise than spoken.

Purposes Of Dialogue

You use dialogue for many reasons beyond the simple fact that your plot calls for a conversation at a certain point. Dialogue is a good way to overcome limitations of some of the tools you are using. For example, if you are writing a first person detective story, dialogue is useful in giving your main character (and in turn the reader) important information. It is also useful in imparting backstory information and exposition. Dialogue does the following:

Develops characters. It is their chance to express themselves directly to the reader. Make sure, though, that the voice they use is consistent. If you want to check this, go back through whatever you've written and highlight everything each character says, using different colors for the different characters, then trace each character's dialogue by itself, making sure it is the same voice. Make sure that all your characters don't sound the same. Dialogue can reveal motivation, which is critical to character. Remember, though, just like in real life, you have to consider whether what a person says is the truth.

One thing you can do to check for consistency with your various characters' dialogue is to highlight each one differently on a print out and then just check that color throughout the entire book.

Dialogue advances the plot. It can sharpen conflict between characters. Since every scene needs conflict, an argument is a way to develop that conflict.

Another thing it can be used for is to ***control the pace*** of the story. Sometimes if you are going full speed ahead with action, dialogue can be a good way to slow things down a little and give the reader a breather. You can do the opposite and pick up the pace of a story with snappy dialogue.

Movies tend to beat dialogue to death, always searching for that greater line. Who can forget Clint Eastwood's "Go ahead, make my day."? While your dialogue should keep the readers' attention, don't beat them to death with stilted dialogue.

Dialogue must fit the characters but try to avoid excessive slang as it usually interrupts the smoothness even though it is natural for that character and locale. Think about it: the reader is going along, your smooth prose has them absorbed in the story, and all of sudden the writing changes to slang. It can be disconcerting. Again there are places where it works, but understand what the disadvantage is and weigh it before using.

I liken this to going to see a play by Shakespeare and not being able to see the stage, but only being able to hear. So you have a friend sitting next to you who describes all the action. I don't know about you, but it takes me several minutes to get used to listening to 'olde English'. But what if my friend is describing the scene in 'new' English to me? Would I be able to keep track of everything?

Don't overuse dialogue. Even in a screenplay, half the page should be action. If your book starts to exceed fifty percent dialogue you might have too much, although, as usual there are exceptions to this.

Dialogue Guidelines
Weave in silence
Weave in action
Weave in setting
Have conflict
Cut words to a minimum
Your choice on slang/dialect

Dialogue tags
A dialogue tag is any words you use to indicate who is speaking. A tendency is to feel that you have to use terms such as *he exclaimed; she gasped; he shrieked;* etc. etc., to make up for your lack of tone, gestures, etc. It can, and often is, be overdone. I noticed an interesting thing while reading Larry McMurtry's *Lonesome Dove:* in almost every instance of dialogue, he just simply wrote the word *said.* Seemed to work for him. Use strong *dialogue tags* when absolutely necessary, but don't overdo it or it will take away from the words themselves. This is a very common mistake among new writers. *Said* is noted but not noticed. You only get to use a unique dialogue tag like *shrieked* once in the entire book. The reader will subconsciously connect the second shriek to the first and it will jar them.

The placement of the dialogue tag is also important. It should be either at the front, middle, or end of the first sentence of dialogue. Don't have an entire paragraph of dialogue and then at the end of the fifth sentence put a comma and quotations marks and *Joe said.* If you do that, the reader spends all five sentences wondering exactly who is speaking.

If you have more than one male in a scene you can't use "he said" even if in the context of the writing it's pretty evident who is speaking. Same with more than one female. Also, don't have bystanders who you forget about. I've read scenes with three people in them, where one says nothing and sort of fades into nothingness by the end, then startlingly reappears at the end of the dialogue. That's called having a secret agent on stage.

Dialogue is usually much shorter in a novel than it would be in real life. There are several reasons for that but mostly it is because people expend numerous words in real life to make a point. Words that in print would quickly cause the reader to lose interest.

An example of how difficult it is to write dialogue is an online chat room. When people are forced to use only the words, communication often breaks down and misunderstandings abound. In the manner, read a court transcript and see how difficult some parts are to follow.

Dialogue Tag Help
Use setting--keep the reader oriented

Use action--move the plot forward

Put the tag at the beginning of, middle, or end of the first sentence if there is a paragraph of dialogue

Don't have unattributed dialogue if more than two people in a scene

Beware pronoun confusion—two of same sex

Don't be stilted

Use contractions

Quotation marks for thoughts

Two characters switching, reorient

Banter
Is gentle conflict.

It's a ping-pong game where you want your shot returned, not to win, but to keep playing.

Should be paced to fit characters.

Can do multiple banters at the same time if you are very skilled. I believe some of the best scenes in the books I co-wrote are when Jenny's heroine carries on multiple conversations, such as the Wonderwear party in *Don't Look Down*.

Other points to consider on dialogue

I said above that you can use dialogue to give expository information but if you do it so obviously, then guess what—the reader will notice and be distracted. This is also true of films. For example, Jim turns to his wife Marge and says: "Gee, Marge, your uncle Bill, the famous artist, is coming from his home in France, to visit us next week." Now, you did give the reader important information about Bill here: that he's a famous artist, Marge's uncle, and he lives in France. But. Don't you think that Marge would know her own uncle is an artist and lives in France? This is called "As you know" dialogue. Any time you use that phrase, you're info-dumping on the reader.

Although dialogue in a novel is usually much more concise and to the point than dialogue in real life, be sure it doesn't appeared stilted or formal. Your characters can use contractions.

While you should be wary of dialogue tags, there are times you have to get across more emotion or attitude than the words themselves can convey. Make up for the lack with action and setting rather than dialogue tags. Also, there are times in extended conversations where the reader can get so caught up in the dialogue they lose track of where the characters are and the environment around the people. Occasionally, you should throw in a little bit of action in the midst of your dialogue. For example, when you are talking to someone on the phone, do you sit totally still? Or do you move about? Play racquetball while on your portable? When you talk to your boss, does he sit still on the other side of his desk and respond to your questions like

Data on *Star Trek: The Next Generation*? Keep the reader oriented to the place the characters speaking are in, and what they are doing. You can give more emphasis to your dialogue by having them make movements or gestures but don't overdo it.

You can use dialogue to give expository information that is necessary for the story but beware of slowing your action down too much with this. This is a place where you must consider using your author's voice to give narrative information instead of contriving scenes where your characters have to sit around and discuss something in order to give that information to the reader.

If you have only two characters in a scene, the reader knows when they hit an end quotation mark that they are going to the other character; however, you should only do about three or four exchanges like that before reorienting the reader as to who is speaking. We've all read scenes where we had to go back up and count the end quote marks to figure out who is talking. Don't make the reader work that hard.

Keep the story flowing. Don't stop the story to let your characters have a discussion and then jump-start it at the end of the discussion.

Setting

Setting is both time and place. Most people think first of place and don't consider time. Yet many bestselling books take an idea that has been done and move it to another time and they have a completely different story.

For example, David Milch went to HBO and pitched an idea and story

Idea: A miniseries about a city that has no police force; no formal law and order.

Story: Ancient Rome, which had no police, but rather relied on the street gangs being paid off to enforce law.

Unfortunately for him, HBO had a mini-series in production at the time: *Rome*.

Did that stop Milch? No. He went home, researched, thought hard, and went back to HBO with the same idea, but a different time and place: He wanted to set the same idea in a town called *Deadwod* in 1876.

Some things to consider when choosing a setting

Does it create conflict as an antagonist, a foil?

Does it create mood, and give sensory experience?

Does it push plot and change character?

Does it reflect the POV character's reality?

Does it bring uniqueness to your story?

Why did you choose these settings?

Setting is mood

Go to the bookstore and open up a bunch of books and read the first line. A "dark and stormy night" is a cliché because clichés are truisms. You will find many opening sentences have something to do with setting and evoking an emotion in the reader. There are some famous writers who say you should never open a book with setting. That's fine for them. It really depends how important the setting is to the story. If the setting is the predominant factor in tone in the story, then opening with it makes sense. There are no rules, only tools.

Setting can be a character in your story, although I don't believe it should be the antagonist. Many think the antagonist in Jon Krakauer's *Into Thin Air* is Mount Everest and the weather. I disagree. I believe the antagonist was the characters themselves. Who climbs a mountain where the fact is one out of six die? Play Russian roulette and save yourself a lot of time, cost and effort. The same with *The Perfect Storm*. The storm doesn't care about the fishermen. It has no concrete goal and no motivation. It just is. The problem is the fishermen who push on when they should turn back.

And think, in both those stories, there were characters who wanted to push forward and those who wanted to turn back. Thus, you can externalize this conflict and make it personal between characters, which is the essence to a good story.

Some authors are known for books set in a certain place. Dennis Lehane and Boston. Michael Connolly and LA. Pat Conroy and the Low Country.

Some genres rely more heavily on setting than others. In science fiction, fantasy and paranormal you have to world-build. You must know everything about your new world. The reader doesn't necessarily need it. You must have rules for your world just like we have rules in our world. One of the greatest examples of world-building in fiction is Frank Herbert's *Dune*.

However--you knew there was a however coming didn't you? However, like everything else, you just can't slam the brakes on your plot and wax eloquently about how magic works in your new world. You explain magic as it comes up. When the reader absolutely needs to know about it.

How much is too much detail? If you can take it out and the reader who knows nothing about your story other than what he's read so far doesn't miss it and doesn't need it.

Next time you're sitting watching your favorite sitcom or TV drama pay a little attention when the scene shifts. Every time the scene shifts to a new locale, don't they show the outside of the building for a second or so before moving inside? Ever wonder why the director does that? They do it to orient you as the viewer.

As a writer, you have to do this too, when you shift settings and start a new scene. I call doing this: "set", short for "set the scene". When you start a new chapter or change perspective you have to relatively quickly (in the first two paragraphs) orient the reader as to:

Where is this located?

When in the timeline is this, especially in regard to the previous scene?

What is the point of view, and if it is a character's in third limited, which character?

Who is on stage?

SETTING EXERCISE: *Where is your story set? When is your story set?*

Special Operations Tactic: Area Study

Study completely the environment in which your story will take place. I like to 'walk the terrain'. It's something I learned in the military. Maps and satellite imagery are all right, but there is nothing like being there when it is possible. When writing *Duty, Honor, Country A Novel of West Point to The Civil War* I went to many battlefields to get an over all feel for the layout. The emotional impact of being at these battlefields shows up in the writing, making it a more compelling read.

Area Study

Get the five senses involved

Do it first hand

Second hand via video, area experts

Keep track of distances

Use maps

Use floor diagrams

Keep track of time of day

Keep track of time around the world

SETTING EXERCISE: *What mood do you want to evoke with setting?*

Writing Sex and Violence

Sex

The hit TV show Seinfeld has covered every possible topic, including sex. Here is the dialogue from the Yada, Yada episode about sex:

George: *You don't think she would yada, yada sex?*

Elaine: *(raises hand) I've yada yadaed sex.*

George: *Really?*

Elaine: *Yeah, I met this lawyer, we went to dinner, I had the lobster bisque, we went back to my apartment, yada, yada, yada, I never heard from him again.*

Jerry: *But you yada, yadaed over the best part!*

Elaine: *No, I mentioned the bisque.*

One of my novels was rejected because the editor was really turned off by the first sex scene. I won't get into details—sorry—but there was a disturbing edge to it. There were four total sex scenes that were layered in after the first draft. I was trying to establish the nature of the relationship between the protagonist and his girlfriend.

But I did it badly.

I had been trying to set up the girlfriend as the antagonist in the second book in the series. One of my tenets as a teacher is write each book as a standalone, so I was violating my own rules. The scene itself was so graphic it left the reader wondering how sick were these two people? Well, they were sick in their own rights, but the problem was that readers were not empathetic to my protagonist yet. While they don't have to be "likeable" they must be empathetic and this scene failed to give the reader anything to hold on to, so I rewrote.

Remember *American Psycho*? Info dump coming: Simon & Schuster originally bought the book but refused to publish it because of the graphic violence and sex so it went to Vintage. The author received death threats and hate mail. Gloria Steinem opposed the book because of the violence toward women. Interestingly, Steinem is the stepmother of Christian Bale who portrayed the protagonist in the movie version.

Sex scenes have to have purpose and move your story forward. Sex for the sake of sex is just that...sex. A sex scene is an interesting way to show small changes in our characters at a deeper level. Actions speak louder than words. A sex scene where the hero and heroine are intimate for the first time could be a way to show insecurities and fears.

While the sex is the action, the scene itself is not about sex, but about character arc and development and there needs to be conflict. This might not happen on an external level, but there must be some conflict on an internal level or you don't need the scene.

In my early books when people had sex, someone died shortly afterward, much like in a horror movie. (Actually, I didn't want the guy to have to make small talk afterwards.)

Do you have to write a sex scene? No. If the book requires one to show something about character and plot, then write the sex, otherwise, forget about it.

What is considered too graphic? It all depends on story, character, and genre. If you are writing a sweet romance, sex probably won't be on the page. If you are writing a romantic suspense novel there is a good chance your characters will have sex.

Whose POV should be used? The POV of the story.

Men and woman do approach sex differently and this can be something to use for character in your books. For men, when sex is over, it's over. For women it's usually just the beginning. Key here is character and expectations. You have to be consistent with character.

Bottom line, write your book.

Violence

I watched *Mission Impossible III* and, in my opinion, it was an excellent example of filming lousy action. I particularly dislike the way explosions are used as ways to 'propel' Tom Cruise forward. They don't hurt him, they move him. And when he falls to the end of a steel cable and is abruptly halted, unlike mere mortals whose back would be broken (ropes are used for climbing because they have at least 1/3 give if you have a fall), Tom motors on. And the bad guys blow up and kill all the other people in all the other cars, but not Tom in his car. Lucky guy. As you can tell, you don't want to watch an action movie with me. Besides being unrealistic, it violated something I think is very important for action scenes: timing.

Action should play out in real time. Not slow motion. If a character fires a gun, the bullet should land in the same sentence or the next sentence. Not two pages later while the guy who shot the gun has a sudden memory of his pet kitten Bubbles and how much he misses her because the bad guy killed her a year ago and how the hero has spent every waking second tracking the SOB and now, yes, now it's finally payback, but, dang, he sure misses Bubbles and he remembers when he found Bubbles, wet and bedraggled on the side of the road while strolling through Central Park with Holly Golightly and, boy, Holly, wasn't she something, cause—and then the bullet lands and the reader forgot he even fired it.

The purpose of a violent action scene is the same as a sex scene. No, not that. You:

Show character through conflict

Move the plot

Raise the stakes

It has meaning within the story and isn't gratuitous

Why do people fight? What can motivate someone to violence? What most people don't understand, is that people often revert to violence because they're afraid. That bully? He's acting the way he is because of fear.

In combat, fear can easily incapacitate. SLA Marshall claimed a very low percent of soldiers actually fired their weapons in combat. His data has been disputed but one of the major purposes of training is to get soldiers to overcome fear and fight. A large percentage of officers in the Army go through Airborne training, yet there is only one Airborne Division, the 82nd, and most won't be going there. So why? To get them to overcome fear and step out of a perfectly good airplane.

Most of what you see in movies isn't real. As my first platoon sergeant in the First Cavalry Division told me: there are two firing positions: the prone and the flying prone (the latter when you get shot at and you aren't already prone—you dive for it).

Most soldiers fight for their buddies. Not God or country.

Point of view is key in action scenes. A thriller is hard to write in first person. It's been done, but the action scenes are difficult because your camera is locked down to one participant in the scene. The person who knows the least about what's going on in combat is the poor soldier in the middle of it.

Omniscient works well for action, particularly large action scenes. Because you can put the camera up high and show the big picture.

In *Agnes And The Hitman* I have an action scene where Moot makes a cameo appearance. If you don't know who Moot is, read *Don't Look Down*. I have a protagonist: Shane. A scene antagonist: Rocko. A setting: in the swamp. Shane is trying to get information out of Rocko. Except, as his name indicates, Rocko isn't too bright. The scene builds slowly, and ends fast. With extreme violence. It moves the plot because Shane does find out some important information. It has humor because, well, Rocko aint too bright. It has violence because Moot is hungry and smells blood in the water. The violence happens fast.

Remember, also, the plan only lasts up to LD/LC (Line of departure, line of contact). That's the line drawn on the map where, after you synchronize your watches, the order says you will cross the LD/LC at 0342 hours, precisely. And it's where the chance of making contact with the enemy begins. You can have the greatest plan, but things go wrong. This is where you can add some interesting twists. Shane didn't expect Moot to be lolling around in the above action scene. So his plan kind of got interrupted.

What does the violence say about your characters who are involved in it?

In *Don't Look Down* in the bar fight, it says something about Bryce that he is at least willing to try to fight. It says something about Wilder how he quickly ends the fight without escalating to deadly violence. And how he reacts after the fight.

I once blogged a rant about *A History of Violence* where I felt the hero was unredeemable. I also feel that way about the ending of *MI III*. Spoiler alert. Tom is strolling across the bridge with his wife after escaping the bad guy and she's like: Now what exactly do you do for a living? Him: I'm in IMF. Her: What's that? Him: The Impossible Mission Force. Her: You're joking? Him: No. Her: I Love you. She puts her arm around him and they go off to live happily ever after.

Let me ask you something: you marry someone and they tell you they're a traveling shoe salesman. Then you get kidnapped by some lunatic, dragged halfway around the world, he has a gun to your head and is going to kill you. You end up having to shoot a couple of people (one of whom conveniently brings the weapon of mass destruction with him to drop in front of you while dying), then have to resuscitate you husband whose heart has stopped because he just electrocuted himself to turn off the bomb he has in his brain and after all is said and done he's: Ah honey, I'm not a shoe salesman, I'm in the Impossible Mission Force.

Most women I know wouldn't go 'I love you.' If, like Agnes, they had a frying pan handy, they'd be whacking him over the head.

So. Violence. Only as a last resort. Real time. It has to make sense and be integral to the plot. It indicates something to your readers about the characters and how they act.

Defeating Writer's Block

On the whole, I have to honestly say most often when I grind to a halt, I am committing the sin of procrastination rather than my creative juices have run dry.

What Is Writer's Block?

Laziness.

95% of the time. Yep. Get out the bum glue.

Right brain/left brain conflict.

Your right brain is your creative side. Your left brain is the editorial side. Whichever one is dominant that morning, will determine whether you feel you wrote brilliance or dreck the previous day as you re-read it. Ignore both and just write. It will turn out the same.

Subconscious telling you to stop.

This is the 5%. This is when you feel bad for several days about the way the book is going. Something is wrong and you need to put the brakes on and figure out what you're screwing up.

Ways To Overcome The "Block"

Have a good outline. Since you've already poured a lot of creativity into your outline, you can usually keep pushing ahead.

As the commercial says: Just do it. Just write. It might be awful but at least it's something other than a blank page.

Work on something else for a while. Looking up at my work board, right now I have (remember this example is from a while back, but you get the idea):

One manuscript on the market at a publisher.

A screenplay getting read by a producer for rewrite.

Two concepts for third books to follow two two-book contracts with major publishers that need to be outlined in time for a new contract.

Two new ideas that I'm researching and beginning to outline.

Two manuscripts getting edited at publishing houses and due back in the next month for more work.

As you can tell, I have so much else going on that I value the time I can spend focused on simply writing. But if I do get a block, I have plenty of other things to work on, including this book. It has been written over a fifteen-year span now going from about eleven manuscript pages on the first draft to over three hundred and fifty.

If you are sure that you need to pause to rethink where your novel is heading, give what you have to someone for feedback. Talk to other people. Clear you head. Free associate. Turn everything in your novel around and look at it from another perspective. Do some more research. Scream. Pound your forehead into your keyboard. Look back through the manuscript for those subconscious seeds you've planted that you can now cultivate and harvest to keep the book moving forward and tighten it down.

Then write.

The Danger of Perfectionism

You could edit out subconscious seeds if you are constantly editing yourself. Just write and get to the end of the first draft. Then work on editing.

You might end up cutting perfectly edited work that you now have wasted time on.

Some people do a lot of rewriting to avoid moving forward. If you enjoy the process more than the end result, you will have a tendency to do this.

Nothing is ever done: sometimes you just have to stop

Bottom line: the next book will be better

Show Don't Tell and Symbolism

You've Heard It, What Does It Mean?

If you've ever attended a writing class or conference, "Show, don't tell" has fallen upon your ears again and again. What exactly does it mean?

First, let me say that it isn't completely true all the time. There are indeed times in a novel when you should tell. In fact, telling is one of the advantages a novelist has over a screenwriter who must stay completely in the showing mode.

Also, the line between showing and telling is non-existent at times. It's a sliding scale. At one end (telling) is pure exposition; at the other end (showing) is dramatization. Telling tends to summarize information, giving it secondhand. Showing allows you to see, hear, feel, smell and taste, first-hand.

Some things to keep in mind when considering whether to show or tell.

Don't Do Information Dumps

Too often people lead with information rather than plot. Information should only be given to the reader when it is absolutely necessary *at that moment* for the reader to understand the plot. Too many writers give information too soon and the reader doesn't know why they are being given this material.

Also, many people open a book with a nice opening line or paragraph and then suddenly go into memory or flashback or info-dump. My recommendation is that if you have a memory or flashback in your opening chapter, you are starting the book in the wrong place.

Match The Two To The Inherent Pace Of Your Story

If you have a fast-moving thriller, a lot of telling can really slow down the story. On the other hand, if you are writing a multi-generational family saga, there will probably be a lot of telling. Also, mix the two. If the reader gets too much telling, they might get bored; too much action might overwhelm. You can balance the story by using both.

Always Show Action

Don't have your action occur 'off-stage'. Summarized action is boring. Play action out in real time in front of the reader.

Always Show The Climax Of The Book
And have your protagonist and antagonist in the scene.

Symbolism
Remember those literature classes where the teacher went on about Faulkner's use of the color yellow in *Soldier's Pay?* Did they call it symbolism?

The example I'm going to use is Richard Russo's superb book *Nobody's Fool.* It was also made into an excellent movie, from which Paul Newman was nominated for an Oscar.

The opening of the book is several pages spent on the old trees overlooking the main street in the town the story is set in. The trees were once the pride of main street but now they are old and diseased and the people who live there fear them, that an unexpected branch will collapse on their house or them. This foreshadows a large part of the story. The trees are a symbol for the way the entire town has become.

Then there is the symbol for conflict. The main character, Sully, has a running feud with a man he worked for, Carl. So Sully steals Carl's new snow blower. And Carl steals it back. And Sully steals it once more. And in the process Sully accidently poisons Carl's dog, which Carl gives to Sully at the end, a symbol of Sully having changed because he now can take care of something/someone else.

Some symbols are most blunt. Sully hates his departed father. Every time he drives by the cemetery where his father is buried, Sully gives the grave the finger.

Symbolism, to tie it in with the first part of this chapter, is how we *show* things to the reader, rather than tell them.

Tool 8: After the First Draft

Getting Feedback

Writers Groups

This is a delicate subject. Many writers swear by their groups. Overall, I'm not that big of a fan unless the group fits certain specific requirements. I lay those out in another book dedicated solely to the subject of writers groups and how to build one that moves forward rather than goes in circles.

Sometimes writers groups are the blind leading the blind. You need a leader in such a group; a leader who is a successful author and experienced and good at controlling the group without letting ego get in the way.

You need a group that moves forward. For novel writers this is particularly hard.

You need a group that is the right size. For novels, more than four or five people starts getting awkward. Can everyone in the group keep up with that many manuscripts? Under three and it's two people staring at each other with their hands over their red pens, ready to draw down on each other. Sometimes, I think it's much better for a novelist to have . . .

Beta Readers

I've always had beta readers; a couple of people who I trust to read the manuscript from beginning to end when I've completed it. Many writers have a problem with beta readers. The problem isn't what the beta readers have to say, the problem is whether we as writers are willing to listen to them? I've 'critiqued' a lot of writers over the years and most have been open to comments. However, about one in five 'fights' back. They start explaining things with the basic philosophy of *well, you didn't get it.* My reply is usually, *you're right, I didn't.* The reality is it's not the reader's job to *get it.* It's the writers job to rewrite so the reader gets it. Got it?

I like the idea of beta readers being readers and not other writers. Writers tend to be too picky. Also, they can resent writing that is better than their own.

How many beta readers should you have? Three or four is a good number. More than that and you end up with too many cooks in the kitchen. You are the sole cook. Using only one reader is dangerous too. It's good sometimes to have opposing views. Beta readers will let you know what they see purely from the writing.

Book Doctors

This is a personal choice but I've never had an agent or editor come back with feedback that I wasn't already aware of on some level. A good book doctor costs A LOT. When I used to look at people's material, I told them I could figure out 95% of what was going on from just seeing their query letter (idea), synopsis (story) and first ten pages. The pages gave me information about their writing style, point of view, etc. etc. I didn't need to read the next 390 pages to keep making the same comments.

Bottom line with book doctors: you get what you pay for.

Agent Feedback

Normally this consists of a one-page letter. If an agent has to write more than that, they probably aren't going to work with you. You need an agent you can trust. And listen carefully to their feedback, because they see the manuscript in terms of whether they can sell it or not.

When getting this feedback, as well as any other feedback, you have to divine the difference between being upset because you screwed up and it needs work or believing what you did was right and you want to stick to your guns. Usually you're wrong.

Editorial Feedback

My experience in this area has ranged from none to a 14 pages single-spaced letter. Both extremes were not good. In this day of self-publishing you definitely need a professional opinion on your manuscript along with help. Again, you get what you pay for.

The most important thing about feedback is being willing to listen. There is a theory that you should cut the part of the book you love the best and there is truth to that. We build our greatest defenses around our greatest weaknesses. You're emotionally attached to some part of your manuscript because you know it doesn't belong but you just love that damn scene or character or paragraph or sentence.

Willingness to change is the #1 trait of successful authors.

The thing to remember about all this feedback is that they can point out problems but rarely can they provide the solutions. It's *your* novel. Sometimes the answer to a problem in chapter 2 lies in changing something in chapter 23.

The big thing to remember is that you don't get to explain outside of the covers of the book. The manuscript has to stand on its own.

Editing

Editing is the nuts and bolts of the words on the page.

I think editing is a right brain, left brain issue. As physiological psychologists will tell you, our nervous system does a switch at the base of the brain, where a right brained person is left-handed and vice versa. Right brained people are considered more creative (generally) while left brained are more logical. Most people consider editing to be a left-brain process, but I think we do our brains a great disservice if we don't trust our right brains. I've seen many struggling writers use their left brain to dominate their right and devastate their writing.

There are two types of editing: story editing (rewriting) and copy editing.

Story Editing

Ask yourself the following questions:

Is there continuity?

Does every sentence and action serve a purpose in the story?

Does the story flow logically?

Why now? Does the initiating event make sense?

Does the story open with the protagonist in conflict with the antagonist or someone linked to the antagonist?

Does your opening establish mood, tone, voice and setting?

Does the reader know what the problem to be solved is?

Does the reader know who your protagonist is?

Do your turning points strip away a layer of motivation for your character AND turn the story in a new direction?

Does the conflict escalate for BOTH protagonist and antagonist?

Is the moment of crisis a fight or flee situation where the choice is not obvious?

Have you closed out all your subplots before the climactic scene, in reverse order that they were introduced?

Is the climactic scene your protagonist and antagonist on stage in conflict until one is utterly defeated?

Does your resolution give an emotional pay-off to the reader?

Is your book as good as you can make it?

These and other questions are the ones you ask when story editing. This is the editing that you need most. By the time you finish a manuscript you have read every word dozens and dozens of times. See how the story *feels.* If you read a lot, then you have a feel for a good story or a bad one.

Give it to a Beta Reader. But beware. A writer cannot have a soft skin. Take criticism and examine it very carefully. If more than two people say the same thing then maybe there is some truth to it. Pick people who read a lot and read the type of book that you are attempting to write.

Ask the following questions when editing:

Do these words have a purpose?

Do they relate to my story?

Is this the time to tell this or should some of it wait?

Is my timeline consistent?

Are my characters consistent?

Are my transitions subtle but clear?

Is this section necessary? Can it be cut without affecting the main story?

Again do not write things just because you think it's interesting or you want to lecture or educate the reader. A useful technique for story editing is to let the manuscript sit for a while (several days to a week or two) to clear your head and then take a relook.

Rewriting

This is a foul word to most writers' ears but an essential one. *Every* manuscript I have had accepted for publication has had to be extensively rewritten. By that I mean that although the original idea stayed the same, something that initially seemed rather vital to the story had to change.

Rewriting is not something that just happens after the first draft is done. It too is an ongoing process. Every fifty pages of manuscript, I print it out and go over it. Every time I change the plot somewhat further on in the manuscript, I have to go back and rewrite everything before to fit the change.

It ain't over when you think it's over. When I complete the first draft of a manuscript, my work on that manuscript is somewhere between 1/2 and 2/3 completed. Too many writers are so glad to have finally completed all those pages that the thought of having to go back and rework the whole thing is blasphemous. But it has to be done.

I'm writing this section because less than a minute ago I got off the phone with my agent and we were discussing three of my manuscripts, which have been languishing in his and my care. We talked about one and he just threw out several ideas and in the course of them I got a few ideas that might help me re-write and get rid of the weak points in the story.

The most important thing for me about rewriting is to be honest. To objectively look at a piece of work (which I, as the author, know quite intimately) and find the flaws. Most of the time I know when I'm writing the flaw that it's a flaw. This is a hard area to explain because a lot of times I work simply on gut feeling about what is wrong and needs to be corrected.

Rewriting can vary from having to completely tear apart the manuscript (thank goodness for computers.) to simply making a few changes here and there. But almost every manuscript needs a rewrite.

I suggest you put away a manuscript for at least a week or two after you finish writing it to allow yourself some mental distance before looking at it again. Too many people are self-publishing too quickly. Give it out for reads and listen to the feedback. However, *don't* make changes simply because someone suggests them if you don't feel they are valid. I've spun my wheels on one manuscript making change after change, and what I was changing was the wrong problem. If there is a problem, I believe as the author, if I am honest and take my time, I can usually find it better than probably anyone else (usually, though, after someone else points out that there is a problem to me).

I just received an 11 page, single-spaced letter of comments from my editor on a manuscript that needs to be re-written. I know what it feels like to attend a writing retreat and get back a critique that tears the manuscript apart and recommends changes, some of them rather major.

My first reaction to such a letter is, of course, negative. I've learned to take a couple of days to let that feeling past. I wrote the previous sentence several years ago. Now, when I get editorial feedback I go through the five emotional stages of change before I open the FedEx package:

Denial: There is no problem with my manuscript!

Anger: How dare you say there's a problem with my manuscript! Who the hell do you think you are?

Bargaining: Okay, maybe there is some problem here, but certainly not as much as you say. Maybe I can fix a few things and it will be all right?

Depression: Crap. I've got to do a lot of work and fix this thing.

Acceptance: Rewrite.

Then go through the comments and the manuscript. The next feeling is one close to despair. It appears an almost insurmountable task

You re-write many times while writing the first draft.

Print out every fifty pages or so

Start over from the beginning if you have been away from the manuscript for a while or something significant has changed

Rewrite for main story arc

Rewrite for character arc

Rewrite to make sure all subplots close out and are supported

Rewrite for symbol and motif consistency

Rewrite to copy edit and make it as clean as possible

Fix anything that doesn't feel right

Killing It—The Ultimate Edit

After attending many writing conferences, I believe that numerous aspiring novelists become too enamored of their first manuscript. If you talk to published authors you will find out that the vast majority did not get their first manuscript published. It was an investment in learning. They moved on to write a second, a third, however many it took to get published. It's a difficult thing, but often you have to take the manuscript and shove it in a drawer, give up on getting it published and move on to writing your next one. You have to take out that trusty .45 pistol and put that thing down.

Most bestselling authors I know killed their first couple of manuscripts before they wrote the one they knew would sell. In these days of self-publishing it might seem harsh to not take the chance and throw it out there, but you might be throwing crap out there and that won't be pretty.

Post-First Draft Feedback

Rewrite for character arcs
Rewrite to tighten down the plot
Rewrite for symbol consistency
Rewrite to cut unnecessary material
Look for conflict in every scene

Copy Editing

This is an ongoing process. Your computer has a spellchecker. I assume you have a reasonable mastery of the written word so this is a matter of putting the time in with a red pencil/pen and paying attention to detail. If you are fortunate enough to be published, you will have professionals go over your work with a fine tooth comb and even then they will miss a few things.

Remember the following basic rules:

Don't repeat words or phrases
Use a style manual
Don't have secret agents

Always know who is doing what to whom or what

The fewer words the better

The bottom line is: Is it clear?

A good technique to help eliminate extra words and to make your writing smoother is to read it aloud and have someone listening with a copy of your manuscript and a red pen. Have them note where your *verbal* reading "edits" the copy. You'll be surprised how much you change what you have written when you have to speak it.

The most important thing to remember about words is: Verbs are power words. Adjectives and adverbs are weaker words that can dress up your work but can also interfere with the smoothness of the writing. Hemmingway is an extreme example of writing using verbs as power words and trying to minimize adjectives and adverbs.

Active Versus Passive Tense

When characters act they are more persuasive than when they react (passive). When characters react they are less sympathetic to the reader.

Try not to overuse words ending in -ing.

For example:

Don was sitting there

Don sat there

The second sentence is more direct and smooth.

Do not repeat words if you can help it—especially uncommon words, because the first time it will go by smoothly but the second time will jar the reader and remind him/her of seeing it before.

Adverbs

Make sure each one is essential. Ask yourself if you can eliminate the need for the adverb by choosing a different verb.

Avoid overusing verbs that end in *-ing*. The primary purpose of an *-ing* verb is to show simultaneity.

Weak verbs. Always see if you can change the word to a more descriptive one.

Avoid vague pronouns. Don't make the reader work to figure out who you are referring to. Always have an antecedent to your pronoun or else it doesn't make sense.

The last word on editing is: Omit all unnecessary words.

When Is The Book Done?

Sometimes you just have to stop.

Sometimes you put it aside

Sometimes you have to kill it

Trust your gut

Tool 9: Your Process

As a new writer, or even a seasoned one, it's important to constantly look at your process. New writers are developing it and seasoned ones are honing it, but the key is to find what works for *you*...not just do what an expert tells you to do.

One of the paradoxes of writing, and something to keep in mind after reading this book: You've been presented with techniques, ideas, and formats that are the "accepted" way of doing things; yet the "accepted" way makes you the same as everyone else who can read a writing book and follow instructions, and your work has to stand out from everyone else's. So how do you do that? How do you do things the *right* way, yet be different, i.e. there are many roads to Oz, which path is yours?

Everything mentioned in this book is a template; do not allow anything to stifle your creativity. Remember the paradox. The best analogy, as mentioned earlier, is that if you were a painter this book is telling you about the paint and the canvas and lighting and perspective, and how to sell your work to a gallery, but ultimately you are the one who has to decide *what* you are going to paint and *how* to paint it. This book introduces you to the tools of writing, their advantages and disadvantages, so that you can wield them effectively.

Understand the tools, and then use your brilliance to figure out a way to change the technique or method to overcome problems and roadblocks. Learn to be original– an artist– with something that's already been done. Also learn so you can mix techniques and methods in innovative ways.

What are the basics of being a writer? The first one is to write a lot. The second, and it actually comes before the first, is to be a voracious reader. The third to understand the craft of writing and have a good reason for everything you do in your manuscript. The fourth is to learn the proper way to do business in the world of publishing, which can be found in *Write It Forward: From Writer to Successful Author*.

The majority of writers fail because while they may have the innate ability and drive, they lack direction and focus and a process. That was a purpose of this book: to allow you to direct your vision into a mode and medium that others will want to buy and read.

A book comes alive in the reader's mind. You use the sole medium of the printed word to get the story from your mind to the reader's. The wonder of writing is to create something out of nothing. Every book started with just an idea in someone's head. Isn't that a fantastic concept?

In my opinion, being a writer is the best job in the world. Every author I know works incredibly hard and when they focus on making money, it's not so they can buy things, it's so they can continue to support their writing.

Being an author is being an artist. Art is a way of expressing concepts, emotions, thoughts, questions—a variety of things to other people.

While much of what we discussed in this book seems mundane, putting it into practice is difficult. Pulling all the pieces together into a coherent whole, is even more difficult. But the payoff when it all comes together is fantastic.

Perfecting Your Process

As I stated in the beginning of this book, there is no right or wrong way to write a book. Your process is everything you do from when the first idea pops into your head, to developing characters and plot, and the actual writing. Process also includes how you go about taking idea to story, editing that story, and starting the circular flow over again with the next book.

A Circular Flow For The Creative Soul

After the idea comes the actual work. I view writing as a continuous four-stage cycle.

Stage 1: The Idea

After the main storyline, you need to know where you are starting each time you sit down to write. Where is the story at that point, and where is it going in the immediate future? I usually do this a chapter or two ahead at a time. Always remember your one sentence original idea. I like to start every day of work by reminding myself of it.

Stage 2: Research

Often I find upon researching an idea that there are many other aspects to the subject that I was not aware of. In many cases research drives the creative train. There is a very thin line between being realistic and telling a story. Real life is sometimes pretty amazing and sometimes you have to bend reality a little for the sake of your story. Bend it too far though, and no one will be interested in sticking with you. Also you must make sure you have internal validity to your story. For example, if you are writing science fiction and have faster than light space travel, you must have certain rules as to how that travel works and you must stay within the boundaries of the rules you set up. Remember the diagram? Research is key to building that background box. I constantly research, pretty much every day, even while I am writing, because it gives more opportunities to develop the plot. Part of research is doing a book dissection.

Stage 3: Writing

Sit down and write. Make sure you have conflict lock. Then start with your outline. Then get into the book itself. Just get it down on paper. It almost always looks awful the first draft. But at least it's written. Give yourself a pat on the back for doing that. Worry about the awful later. Use 'bum glue' as Bryce Courtenay says. There is absolutely no other way to finish a manuscript other than writing it, one word, one sentence, one paragraph, and one chapter at a time.

Stage 4: Editing

Go back and look at what you wrote. Clean it up. Throw it out if it doesn't fit (don't literally throw it out—never, never, never discard something you wrote. You never know when you might need it in another story or after the first draft of the manuscript is done. Label it and save it.) To start my writing day, I usually begin by going back and at least read what I wrote the previous day, cleaning it up as I go. This not only edits the work, but also gets me in the proper groove to continue.

Now I am going to be very honest with you. Unlike most writers (or at least unlike what most writers say) I have no real set routine. Sometimes I wake up and jump right into writing. Sometimes I spend days editing. Sometimes I spend days doing nothing externally, but spinning wheels in my head, trying to figure out what I'm doing with the story (but there are less and less of those days lately because— you got it—I have good outlines.).

There is no typical workday for me other than the fact that I do work at something every single day. I have listed out all sorts of routines and suggestions in this book so far and I have used all of them at one time or another. But don't feel like there is a golden rule. If one day you want to write standing on your head on the New York City subway—then go for it (just be careful—it's a jungle out there.). Sometimes I sit down and outline chapters just like I suggested in the outlining section. Sometimes I don't outline the chapter, I just begin writing it. Do whatever works. But work.

Write It Forward

Quite a bit of what you just read won't make very much sense--or too much sense—to you if you are just beginning to write manuscripts. But reread it every once in a while and you will find that the more you write, the more sense it makes. I read numerous writing books when I first began and got quite frustrated because a lot of it seemed very simple or I didn't agree with some of the things that were said. But I didn't truly understand until I tried writing. Then it all begins clicking into place.

Remember—writing is work. You must put the time and effort into it to succeed. Learn, listen, read and ask a lot of questions. Go to conferences, take workshops and network with other authors regarding the craft of writing. Join writers' groups and organizations. Get a critique group. Write, write and then write some more.

I've laid out the foundation for the writing part of being an author. This is what your career will be built on. However, while you are honing and perfecting your craft, it is also important to study the business.

Write It Forward: From Writer to Successful Author is the sister book to what you have just read. *Write It Forward* will help you understand the business and your changing role in publishing. In the last few years, publishing has changed drastically, opening many new doors and opportunities for today's writer. Understanding yourself and your role in publishing will help you be a successful *Write It Forward*.

So, although I said there is no right or wrong, I will leave you with one simple rule: ***WRITE IT FORWARD***

Appendix 1: Sample Chapter Outline

For Area 51 (Kelly Reynolds; Turcotte; Gullick; Simmons)

Chapter 1:

Nashville/ 9 Nov/ 11 PM/ 0400 Zulu

Kelly Reynolds gets tape and letter in mail from a male reporter friend as she comes home late at night.

She listens to tape—intercepted radio conversation between AF jet pilot participating in Red Flag (US vs. "Soviet" simulation fight out of Nellis AFB) getting caught by tower (Dreamland—Nellis AFB call sign) for violating restricted air space over Area 51. Pilot reports being forced down by strange object, then goes off air suddenly. Male friend says he is going to investigate—will be there on such and such night—the same night she is listening to the tape.

Nellis Air Force Base Range/ 9 Nov/ 10 PM/ 0600 Zulu

Shift to male reporter infilling site 51 in Nevada (will be sent to Dulce later)

The Cube, Area 51/ 9 Nov/ 10:30 PM/ 0630 Zulu

Shift to underground govt building (the Cube= C3= CCC, Command and Control Central) where they pick up the man infilling on IR scope from nearby mountain and track him coming in. Introduce General Gullick; refer to pending Nightscape mission; start recall.

Purpose: introduces Kelly, Area 51 site mystery.

I list the date at the top, putting it in time sequence for the story.

I have the characters who will be in the chapter (which makes me cross-reference to my character summaries.)

I list the events in sequence, giving the major action and where it occurs.

I make notes on key material that must be dealt with later, in other chapters, or already has been dealt with. This is very important to insure continuity of story.

I have a definite start point at the beginning of the event sequence and a definite end-point. I have listed all important events that I need to occur in between.

Perhaps most importantly I give the *purpose* of the chapter. Where does it fit in the overall story? How does it relate to the original idea? This will prevent having extraneous material.

Appendix 2: Example Story Grid

In the Excel sheet below, each row is a scene. I fill this out as I write, writing in new scenes in pen, then typing it up at the end of the day and printing it out for the next day's work.

Column 1 is chapter number.

Column 2 is start page number.

Column 3 is end page number.

Column 4 is the date. Here, I just have date, since it's a historical epic, but in a thriller I might have two columns, with not just date, but also local and Greenwich mean time.

Column 5 is location.

Column 6 is a brief summary of the action and character so that I can be reminded of what happened in each scene. The far right column is where I make notes on things I need to loop to or rewrite.

I also color code scenes, for example using red for scenes focused on my antagonist, yellow for letters that are in scenes or break scenes, etc. You can do a lot of variations of the story grid, with your imagination your only limitation.

Ch	A	B	Date	Place	Event	Notes
	3	5			**West Point 22 Sept 1839 Grant to Coz**	
	6	6			S April 1862 Beauregard to Army of Mississippi	
1	7		27-May-40	Havens	Sherman, King, Cord, Lidia	
		32	27-May-40	WP Havens	Rumble, Grant, Longstreet, Shermn, Cord	
2	33	37	12-Sep-40	WP	Cord cut from Corps, Grant by him, Lyon Buckner	
3	38	58	1-Jan-41	WP	Agrippa, Cord, St George, Longstreet, Grant BIRTH	
4	59		Jun-41	WP	depart, Lydia pregnant-- Cord going to drop letter?	
		78	Summer 41	Arlington	Cord and Lee-Obidiah; slaves; Texas	
5	79		Summer 41	Palatine	Rumble with Violet	
			Summer 41	Shanty	Torture boy	
			Summer 41	Palatine	Rumble with Tiberius	
		92	Summer 41	Vidalia	St. George w Sally Skull	
6	93		Summer 41	Norfolk	Cord w/Obadiah and father	
		103	Summer 41	Charleston	Cordlia, King, appointment	
7	104	113	Aug-41	WP	Lidia in garden	
8	114		Jan-42		Lidia death bed-promise me Agrippa won't join the Corps	
		122	Fall 41	WP	Bury Lidia	
9	123	139	1-Dec-42	Atlantic	USS Somers	
10	140		Jun-43	WP	Grant jumps	
		154	15-May-43	Violet-Rumble		
11	155		Jun-43		Cord jumps York	
		178	Jun-43	WP	Obadiah, St George, shot at Cord	
12	179		Aug-43	Cincinnatti	Grant uniform, Obadiah, meet Grant, St. George	
		185	Sep-43	Palatine	on front porch, Violet Rosalie & Cord	
13	186		Sep-43	Palatine	Seneca, Obadiah, Grant	
			Sep-43	Palatine	Rosalie & Rumble	
		195	Sep-43	Palatine	St. George w Sally Skull	
14	196		May-45	White Haven	Bury bird	
			May-45	WP	Delafield and Rumble-- War coming	
			May-45	White Haven	Grant engaged	more emotion letter Rumble-Violet
		221	Jun-45	St. Louis	Cord, Kit Carson, Grant	
15	222		1-Jul-45	New Orleans	Grant and Rumble vs St George & Skull	
			Oct-45	Great Salt De	Cord, Fremont	
		238	3-Jun-43	Benton to Fremont		
16	239		1-Oct-45	Annapolis	Founding Naval Academy, duel, Bancroft	
			Oct-45	Palatine	Letter from Rumble, John Dyer dead	
		254	Oct-45	Desert	Indian woman, leave food	
WA	266	267	**WAR**	28-Jul-44	CAMP SALUBRITY- GRANT TO JULIA 28	
17	268		8-May-46	Palo Alto	Under fire, Rumble there	
		274	10-May-46	Oregon	Klamath Village massacre	
18	275	280	Jun-46	Palatine	St George & Sally Skull at statue	
19	281	287	28-Jun-46	San Francisco	Execution San Fran	
20	288		23-Sep-46	Monterrey	Grant runs gauntlet	
			12-Aug-46		Violet-Rumble	more emotion
		309	25-Sep-46		Grant-Julia	
21	310		14-Dec-46	San Luis Obis	Stop firing squad	
			24-Dec-46	Palatine	Teal and Echo-- will come for you	
		322	Jan-47	Banquete	Skull & St. George with Ft. Patrick & Sally	

Excerpt from *Write It Forward: From Writer to Successful Author*

What is Write It Forward?

Publishing is undergoing major changes and these changes are creating new opportunities for writers. *Write It Forward* focuses on educating writers on how to be successful authors and help them conquer their fears. *Write It Forward* is a holistic approach encompassing goals, intent, environment, personality, change, courage, communication and leadership that gives the writer a road map to become a successful author in today's rapidly changing publishing landscape. Many writers become too focused on either the writing or the business end. *Write It Forward* integrates the two putting the control back into the author's hands.

Write It Forward fills a critical gap in the publishing industry paradigm. While there are numerous books and workshops focused on just the writing, this one focuses on the strategies, tactics and mindset a writer needs to develop in order to be a successful author; regardless of the path you choose to publication.

Under the current publishing business model, authors learn by trial and error and networking with other authors. Sometimes it's the blind leading the blind. Given the drastic changes the industry is currently undergoing, the most knowledgeable people admit they have little idea where the industry will be in a year. However, one thing remains constant, writers produce the product and readers consume the product. As we used to say in the Infantry: Lead, follow, or get the hell out of the way. That is a mantra for *Write It Forward*. We must all be leaders.

Authors are the producer of the product in publishing. Agents, editors, publishers and bookstores are currently the primary contractors, processors, and sellers of that product. Online retailers also offer an option that didn't exist just a few years ago. While most agents and editors normally get educated in a career path starting at the bottom of an agency/publishing house, writers, from the moment they sign a contract or self-publish their book, are thrust immediately into the role of author as well as promoter. For the new author it is sink or swim. Unfortunately, with the lack of author training, most sink. First novels have a 90% failure rate, which is simply foolhardy. I submit that the success rate for self-publishing is the same as the success rate for getting an agent, publisher, etc. and breaking out. Either way, this book gives you the tools you will need to succeed regardless of the path you take.

The learning curve to become a successful author is a steep one. In the past, the author might have had years to learn, and when needed, re-invent one's self, but the business is now moving at a much faster pace. It is expected that authors not only have to write the books, but also become promoters of their books. Interestingly enough, Promoter (ESTP) is the complete opposite of Author (INFJ) in the Myers-Briggs personality indicator as we will see under **TOOL FOUR: CHARACTER.** It is difficult to go from one mindset to the other. Not only do you have to be Author and Promoter, you must also be Seller (ESJF).

A key aspect of this book is that just by buying it, you prove you are ahead of the pack because you're willing to learn. When I ran a *Write It Forward* workshop in San Diego one participant said that simply getting on the plane to come take the workshop required her to conquer several of her fears.

EXERCISE: In one sentence, write down your goal for reading this book.

Are you able to define it succinctly? Does it have a positive, action verb? An outcome that is clearly visible? We'll be covering all that in **TOOL ONE: WHAT.**

Can You Walk The Line?
Early in the movie *Walk The Line*, Johnny Cash and his two bandmates go for an audition. I recommend watching the movie and focus-

ing on that scene. Here is the dialogue, with my comments in parentheses and bold.

Johnny Cash singing a cover of an old gospel song—within 15 seconds he is halted:

*Producer **(read agent)**: Hold on. Hold on. I hate to interrupt... but do you guys got something else? I 'm sorry. I can't market gospel **(read generic vampire novel, clichéd thriller, whatever)**. No more.*

Johnny Cash: So that's it?

*Producer: I don't record material **(represent a book)** that doesn't sell, Mr. Cash... and gospel **(a book)** like that doesn't sell.*

*Johnny Cash: Was it the gospel or the way I sing it? **(Was it the book or the writing?)***

Producer: Both.

Johnny Cash: Well, what's wrong with the way I sing it?

Producer: I don't believe you.

Johnny Cash: You saying I don't believe in God?

Bandmate: J.R., come on, let's go.

Johnny Cash: No. I want to understand. I mean, we come down here, we play for a minute... and he tells me I don't believe in God.

Producer: We've already heard that song a hundred times... just like that, just like how you sang it.

*Johnny Cash: Well, you didn't let us bring it home **(you didn't get to my hook, climactic scene, whatever)**.*

*Producer: Bring... bring it home? All right, let's bring it home. If you was hit by a truck and you were lying out in that gutter dying... and you had time to sing one song **(write one book)**, huh, one song... people would remember before you're dirt... one song that would let God know what you felt about your time here on earth... one song that would sum you up... you telling me that's the song you'd sing? That same Jimmie Davis tune we hear on the radio all day? About your peace within and how it's real and how you're gonna shout it? Or would you sing something different? Something real, something* *you felt? Because I'm telling you right now... that's the kind of song people want to hear. That's the kind of song that truly saves people. It ain't got nothing to do with believing in God, Mr. Cash. It has to do with believing in yourself.*

Johnny Cash: Well, I've got a couple songs I wrote in the Air Force. You got anything against the Air Force?

Producer: No.

Johnny Cash: I do.

Bandmate: J.R., whatever you're about to play... we ain't never heard it.

Within fifteen seconds of singing the song he wrote, the producer knows he is looking at a star.

What did Johnny Cash Do?

He tried even though the odds of rejection were high. We hear the scary statistics all the time about the slush pile. You can't let that stop you. There are people who won't query because they're afraid of rejection. In essence, they've just rejected themselves. I heard a very weird statistic recently that 90% of people who have a one-on-one with an agent at a conference and are requested to send in their material, never do. There are many reasons for this, but the #1 barrier is fear. Why even do the one-on-one if you are never going to follow through?

Beyond that, we are witnessing the end of agenting and publishing as it has been known for decades. It's an exciting new world out there and the author who is willing to put herself out there with courage, has better chances than ever before of succeeding because she controls more of the process of getting the book into the reader's hands.

Johnny Cash walked in the door even though he was afraid. We're going to discuss fear a lot in this book. We're also going to discuss ways you can overcome fears.

He went even though his wife didn't think he had it. There is a scene earlier where he and his band-mates are on the porch playing and Cash's wife storms off and locks herself in the bathroom. She tells him he's wasting his time and he needs to get a *real job*. Some of us have heard the same thing, haven't we?

He stayed after being rejected. Most people think rejection is the end. It's actually a beginning. Use rejection as motivation. Rejection is an inevitable part of a writer's life.

He got hit with a double rejection. Not only was he told that the song wasn't good, but his singing wasn't good either. How would you feel if someone told you not only was the book not good, your writing wasn't either?

Even though he was angry, he was respectful. Lashing out, no matter how badly we want to do it, rarely brings us positive results.

He asked questions. I watch people pitch agents at conferences and many rarely ask questions. They're so focused on pitching they aren't using the time as a valuable learning experience. When Cash asked what was wrong, he got a response that allowed him to focus.

He listened. I once got some other rejections on a manuscript. Looking back, I remember my agent making a comment two years previously when I was first talking about the idea. I didn't listen carefully enough to what she was really saying, because in retrospect, what every editor said in the rejection letter was what she had said two years ago. We're going to cover communication in **TOOL SEVEN**. Listening for the real message is a key skill successful people have.

He used his **PLATFORM** and tried again. We're always hearing the buzzword Platform. A lot of people feel they don't have one. You do. If you watch the movie, note the look on Cash's face when he's singing the gospel song about his **Peace Within**. He's not peaceful. He's angry. That's his character arc in the movie, finding peace within. So when he finally sings the song he wrote, he's singing an angry song. Because his platform right then is anger: over the death of his brother; the fact his father blamed him for it; and he hated his time in the Air Force, being away from his girlfriend. Basically, he used his real self and mined his emotions. That's your platform.

He conquered his **FEAR**. He not only walked in, he stayed, and he succeeded.

He **CHANGED**. He walked in with one plan, but when it didn't work, he quickly changed that plan.

EXERCISE: Record the one thing you fear the most as a writer?

Here is a very interesting question that writers should ask themselves:

I will do whatever it takes to succeed as a writer, except don't ask me to do . . .

Whatever completes that sentence is your greatest fear as a writer. This question is a great way of finding the one fear that is crippling you. We must attack the ambush, which I will discuss under **COURAGE**.

What is that nagging thing you know you ought to do, but just can't get yourself to do? Is it a craft problem? A business problem? Promotion? Networking? Committing the time to finish your book? Asking for help?

For me, it's rewriting and focusing after the first draft is done. I've always said I've never had an editor or agent come back with a comment on something I wasn't already aware of. Thus, I need to focus and make sure they can't come back with those comments I am aware of. I also have to promote and market better than I have been in the past. As writers, we tend to dislike that part of our job. But it is PART of the job.

EXERCISE THREE: Finish this statement: I'll do whatever it takes to succeed as a writer, just don't ask me to . . .

What Am I Going to Do?

In tough times, it's the tough who succeed. The Green Berets are mentally and emotionally the toughest soldiers in the military. The first thing you'll sense when you meet a Green Beret is that they exude confidence. It's a palpable sensation. They have confidence in themselves, their team, their unit and Special Forces.

How did they become this way?

They **CHANGED**. After all, that's what this is all about. You wouldn't have picked this book up if there wasn't something in your writing life you wanted to change. This book will teach you the path to be able to change and go from writer to author.

There are the nine **TOOLS** in **WHO DARES WINS** and by reading this book you will gain the insight and knowledge to change the same way Special Forces soldiers go from being regular soldiers to being the best. This book gives you a comprehensive plan to build self-confidence so you can conquer fear and succeed as a writer.

The definition of confidence is trust in a person or thing. A feeling of assurance.

Do you want confidence in all aspects of your writing life?

You have goals in your writing life. You want to achieve things. For most of you, the largest obstacle to your success is fear. This book brings you templates and tactics used by the US Army's Green Berets to conquer fear, build confidence and succeed.

But before you start, you have to ask yourself one very important question:

Do you want to change?

It's that simple. Change is extremely difficult, for many different reasons, which will be covered in this book. The good news is, experts have blazed the way for you and you can use their lessons learned and the techniques they developed. I've taught thousands of writers over the last couple of decades and the biggest problem most have is they are not willing to change.

Do you want a life ruled by fear, or do you want to live to the fullest, confident in yourself?

A successful person can make decisions and take action in the face of fear. The successful are head and shoulders above their peers and competition. They accomplish their goals, have pride in themselves, and find a way to achieve what they want in life. The successful writer takes chances and succeeds. The successful writer embraces the changing world of publishing and uses those changes to their advantage.

FEAR is the number one barrier that keeps you rooted in the mundane and ordinary. It is the primary obstacle to achieving your dreams as a writer. Successful people take action despite their fears. As you'll discover as you read, it is not a question of ignoring fear, but rather the opposite: you must factor fear into your writing life and deal with it.

A lot of what you will learn in this book seems common sense. Some will also be counter-intuitive. We make repeated mistakes without learning from them. This book teaches you how to focus, learn from errors, and not repeat them. Since we all make mistakes, the positive news is that correspondingly there are ways we can improve. We are emotional creatures, and most often our emotions overrule our common sense. Intellectually, our subconscious overpowers our conscious. So we will focus on trying to find the real reasons why we do things, which are often right in front of us, but we are blind to. We will spend quite a bit of time trying to determine blind spots, which are often the roots of our fears.

A lot of what is covered is using my experience as an example. I'm going to give you snippets from my writing career—what worked, what didn't work. From this you will see how I learned all this material. Hopefully, you won't make the same mistakes I did. One advantage is that I have experience in both traditional and non-traditional publishing. My first novel came out in 1991 and I have had over 40 books traditionally published since then. In 2010 I formed Who Dares Wins Publishing with Jen Talty and we now have over 30 books published and have gained considerable experience concerning eBooks, Print-On-Demand and non-traditional publishing. The future of publishing is not going to be a straight and narrow path, but rather a byzantine winding trail with as many opportunities as there are dangers.

This book will show you how to use the strategic tools. Strategic is the big picture. For example, in **TOOL ONE**, we're going to talk about your single strategic goal as a writer. You will have one strategic goal, stated in one sentence, with an active verb.

This book will show you how to use the supporting tools. Supporting is everything that falls under strategic. You have to align everything you do tactically in order to achieve your strategic goals.

Write It Forward is broken down into three areas from the title of the book *Who Dares Wins: The Green Beret Way To Conquer Fear And Succeed* (Pocket 2009), with three steps in each, that I managed to get down to one word each (even beginning with the same letter in each area):

Overview of the *Write It Forward* Program and The Circle of Success

AREA ONE: WINS
TOOL ONE: WHAT specifically do you want to achieve with your writing?

TOOL TWO: WHY do you want to achieve these particular goals?

TOOL THREE: WHERE will sustained change occur?

AREA TWO: WHO
TOOL FOUR: Understand **CHARACTER.**

TOOL FIVE: What is **CHANGE**, and how do you accomplish it?

TOOL SIX: How do you build the **COURAGE** to change?

AREA THREE: DARES
TOOL SEVEN: COMMUNICATE your change to the world.

TOOL EIGHT: Take COMMAND of your change.

TOOL NINE: COMPLETE the Circle of Success and change.

Non-Fiction By Bob Mayer

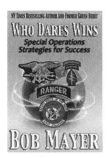

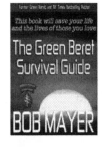

Books By Bob Mayer And Jen Talty

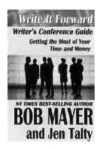

Other Books By Bob Mayer

"Thelma and Louise go clandestine." *Kirkus Reviews on Bodyguard of Lies*

" . . .delivers top-notch action and adventure, creating a full cast of lethal operatives armed with all the latest weaponry. Excellent writing and well-drawn, appealing characters help make this another taut, crackling read." *Publishers Weekly*

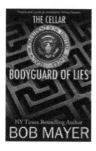 

"Fascinating, imaginative and nerve-wracking." *Kirkus Reviews*

The Presidential Series By Bob Mayer

COMING 5 November

The Green Beret Series

"Mayer has stretched the limits of the military action novel. Synbat is also a gripping detective story and an intriguing science fiction thriller. Mayer brings an accurate and meticulous depiction of military to this book which greatly enhances its credibility." *Assembly*

"Will leave you spellbound. Mayer's long suit is detail, giving the reader an in-depth view of the inner workings of the Green Machine." *Book News*

"Mayer keeps story and characters firmly under control. The venal motives of the scientists and military bureaucracy are tellingly contrasted with the idealism of the soldiers. A treat for military fiction readers." *Publishers Weekly*

"Sinewy writing enhances this already potent action fix. An adrenaline cocktail from start to finish." *Kirkus Reviews*

Historical Fiction By Bob Mayer

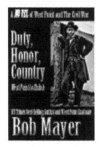